Something Happens, Sometimes Here:

Contemporary Lincolnshire Poetry

Something Happens, Sometimes Here:

Contemporary Lincolnshire Poetry

edited by
Rory Waterman

Five Leaves Publications

**Something Happens,
Sometimes Here:**
Contemporary
Lincolnshire Poetry

Edited by Rory Waterman

Published in 2015
by Five Leaves Publications,
14a Long Row, Nottingham NG1 2DH
www.fiveleaves.co.uk
www.fiveleavesbookshop.co.uk

ISBN 978-1-010170-22-9

Five Leaves is represented
to the book trade by Turnaround
and distributed by Central Books

Typeset and designed by
Four Sheets Design and Print

Printed in Great Britain

Contents

Kathryn Daszkiewicz

Rory Waterman

William Bedford

David Cooke

Clare Best

Michael Blackburn

Sam Gardiner

Rennie Parker

Acknowledgments   133

Biographical Notes   136

Introduction

The poet most likely to come to mind when one has rare occasion to mention 'Lincolnshire' and 'poetry' in the same sentence is, of course, Tennyson, who grew up in the Lincolnshire Wolds. He left at twenty-eight, but continued occasionally to evoke the 'silent woody places' of his youth — a theme we can see echoed in the work of several poets in this anthology. Another of England's defining Poets Laureate, John Betjeman, for whom 'that lord of landscape' Tennyson was a hero, also celebrated the separateness of the county, and was perhaps only half joking when he addressed the 'Lincolnshire Past, Present and Future Conference' in 1963 and said he'd like to see the place 'with its own flag and for passports to be shown to get in'. We're still waiting for the passports, and it took until October 2005 for the Lincolnshire County Council to unveil a flag, chosen in a popular vote. Then, the same month, the Council conducted a poll: 'Do you like the design of the new Lincolnshire Flag?' Sixty-six per cent said 'No', but almost immediately they were fluttering all over the place anyway, proud and bright, on new flagpoles.

This apparent contradiction says something about the spirit of Lincolnshire, binding together people from what is in some senses a disparate county, in which the residents of Barton-upon-Humber live twice as far from London as those of Stamford. The flag is *ours*, and once we'd forgotten that we didn't like it, and that we'd done perfectly well without it thank you, we found we wanted it, even if nobody else knew what it was.

Lincolnshire is England's second biggest county by area, but is nonetheless both marginalised and marginal. Though not a peninsula, it is to some extent behind geographical borders: the Humber to the north, the North Sea to the east, the Wash and tracts of fen — specifically the Lindsey and Deeping Levels, much of them drained only two hundred years ago — to the south, and the River Trent widening slowly along much of its western periphery. Not many people on the outside seem very often to think of traversing the county's borders or nearly-borders: a recent map claiming to label the United Kingdom according to popular perceptions had 'SPARE BIT OF ENGLAND' plastered directly over what, when I was growing up, might as well have been the *only* bit of England. Poets from elsewhere rarely say anything about the place either: in what is probably its most famous mention in the poetry of the last century, it is reduced to the thin slither of filling in Philip Larkin's ethereal sandwich of 'where sky and Lincolnshire and water meet' — still somewhere 'over there', not quite on, but alongside, a railway journey down eastern England.

Even its own exports can give it short shrift, if they think they have moved on to bigger and better things. The poet Ahren Warner grew up in the county, though in more recent times, according to a book blurb, has rather more glamorously 'divided his time between Paris and London'. 'I occasionally have the misfortune to go back,' he quipped at a reading in 2011, before evoking its apparently hellish flatness. But the poems of Alison Brackenbury, or William Bedford, show us a different response from Lincolnshire's émigré poets: the effect of a subtly unique landscape and life getting under a poet's skin — much as they did for Tennyson almost two centuries ago.

The medieval division of Lincolnshire into three segments or 'parts' was abolished in 1974, but lives on in the names of local government districts: Lindsey, covering the northern half, taking its name from the early Anglo-Saxon kingdom of Lindesege; Kesteven, in the south-west; and Holland, in the south-east, beside the Wash. Each is itself the size of a reasonable county.

10

Lincoln is the county town and only city, with a population of about 100,000, and a skyline dominated by the immense medieval cathedral and castle on their ridge of hill. The county's two other fairly big conurbations, Scunthorpe with its steelworks and the twin towns of Grimsby and Cleethorpes with their docks and amusement arcades respectively, are in the north — the part that was, from 1974 to 1996, in the southern section of the pretend county of Humberside, and to this day is separated from most of the county by not being included in the administrative East Midlands region of England.

The next biggest towns are Grantham and Boston, both with populations close to 40,000; the latter is one of England's most solitary bigger places. But Lincolnshire is essentially rural, impenetrably rural for some, most of it hiding behind the gentle, county-long, north-south fold of the Lincoln Edge escarpment. It is a subtly varied county but also essentially workaday and unglamorous, with its two most distinctive geographical areas being the Fens, stretching from Norfolk and Cambridgeshire into its south-east quarter, and the dimpled Lincolnshire Wolds only occasionally sticking their backs above five hundred feet as they roll unevenly down much of the east. Tourists might like it there if only they could be bothered to visit, but the underpopulated villages of Tennyson's youth — Somersby, Bag Enderby, Ashby Puerorum — appear completely uninterested in luring you.

East from the Wolds, between them and the long line of coast, is the flat area known as the Lincolnshire Marsh, created at a prehistoric time when sea levels were considerably higher and waves rolled over it to buffet the chalk escarpment of the Wolds. Tennyson evoked looking from 'high wold' to 'great plain', and beyond, in 'In Memoriam':

> Calm and deep peace on this high wold,
>   And on these dews that drench the furze.
>   And all the silvery gossamers
> That twinkle into green and gold:

11

Calm and still light on yon great plain
  That sweeps with all its autumn bowers,
  And crowded farms and lessening towers,
To mingle with the bounding main [...].

And all over the place in this county are minor mysteries of loneliness: clumps of ignored and often ancient woodland; overgrown former RAF bases and still-operational ones — more than anywhere else in Britain — where orange windsocks ripple in isolation behind miles of fencing; solid farmhouses and barns; ignored villages with their becks, greens, village halls. Occasionally there is of course a larger village or small market town — Sleaford, Alford, Stamford, Wragby, Spilsby, Saxilby, Bourne, Brigg, Burgh le Marsh — limestone-centred in the east of the county and usually brick-built in the west, where good building stone is less common. The county is scattered liberally with prized churches, too: huge monuments to faith such as Lincoln Cathedral, or the bulky part-Saxon, part-Norman Minster Church of St Mary in Stow in Lindsey, or St James's Church in Louth, which has the tallest medieval parish church spire in England, or St Botolph's in Boston — known locally as 'the Stump', though it has England's tallest medieval tower; but also hundreds of small places of worship, many of great age, some evoked here in poems by Sam Gardiner, Rennie Parker, Joel Stickley, David Cooke.

Almost every country view in Lincolnshire has churches in it, big and small, pointy and squat. This oversize county finally culminates with a gently wavering fifty-mile-long line of often dune-backed sand, each end of it spilling into a vast muddy estuary, and with the odd surprise or distraction along its length: the seals and military decoys making uneasy company with one another at the RAF bombing range at Donna Nook; the brash bingo halls of Cleethorpes, Mablethorpe and Skegness; the desolate, tufted dunes of Theddlethorpe; the rutted mudlands of Gibraltar Point. It is fertile ground for a vivid and separate poetry, whose authors often write largely outside of prevailing trends and movements, consciously or obliviously remote from the centres of influence, and who are often the better for it. In this anthology you will find some of that poetry.

***

The purpose of this book is simply to showcase the work of a handful of intriguing contemporary poets, all of whom have strong connections to Lincolnshire, and to concentrate on their poetry about the county. Five of them do not live in Lincolnshire any more, and two never have, or at least not for more than a few short periods at a time. I make no apology for this. The policy has been to select poems that are set in Lincolnshire, which of course makes the county's people, places and history something of a leitmotif. I have only included poets from whose work I could make fairly substantial selections of relevant poems, rather than picking one or two short pieces. A selection of my own poems is also included at the request of the publishers; I hope these do not seem out of place in such excellent company. Each of the poets has been invited to provide a few words on what Lincolnshire means to them and their poetry, and these statements are included here as introductions to the work.

Lastly, I want to say that this anthology is intentionally intended as a sort of Lincolnshire response to Ian Parks's excellent *Versions of the North: Contemporary Yorkshire Poetry*, published by Five Leaves in 2013. As with the counties themselves, this Lincolnshire book is a bit smaller and has fewer people in it than its Yorkshire counterpart, but gives each of them a little more room. I hope it is not also flatter. In any case, readers of the present volume are encouraged to get hold of the book that inspired it.

Alison Brackenbury

Lincolnshire is my past, and my family's past. My writing name, Brackenbury, comes from my father's family. When I asked my grandfather how many generations had been prize-winning shepherds, he said 'My father was, and his father — and mebbe his father' — My father's family were often tall and blue-eyed (Vikings?), ferocious both in temper and their capacity for work. They spoke their minds fearlessly, but with humour. My voice, and my metres, keep their short 'a's.

My father began work at fourteen as a ploughboy, then worked for over forty years as a farm lorry driver. My mother, the youngest child of a gamekeeper and a house-maid, became a teacher and taught in the local school. I grew up in a village of farmworkers, at, I now feel, the very end of Victorian England. (My shepherd grandfather still used a horse and cart.) One day, I must write more of this, in prose...

I left Lincolnshire first for university, then marriage. I did not want to perch in the country with no link to farming, so settled, close to my work, in a small Gloucestershire town. But I learnt to ride (badly) and continued the traditions of my father's family by keeping unaffordable, shaggy ponies up on the hills, and spending far too much of my time there. As in my Lincolnshire childhood, I haunt field edges or small woods, and listen for lapwings. (I have also re-discovered my passion for the lilting, long-lived songs which my mother's father knew, but my parents' generation despised.)

Gloucestershire is, at first sight, less devastated by farming than the vast arable fields of my Lincolnshire youth. Yet the cocktails of chemicals sprayed on soil and crops (which both my father and grandfather feared and hated) have become even more hurtful to wildlife.

Lincolnshire did not just give me uncomfortable insights into the damage we do daily to, I believe, an almost ruined planet. It still draws me to open skies, and winter stars, and (for brief stays only!) a coastline increasingly exposed to floods. Born in a year of terrible East Coast floods, I remain awed by the power of water and of weather. Our small inland village, still darkened by memories of war in the 1950s, was not Paradise. But I remember its people's frugality, a kindness to neighbours, and a natural, dignified friendliness which I still respect, and greatly miss.

Memory shifts. When I first tried to write about Lincolnshire, it was the men's world, outdoors, often close to animals, which so attracted me. Now I have come to reflect on the Lincolnshire lives of the women in my family, and their legacy to me. These include a plump black notebook of handwritten recipes from my father's mother, an Edwardian cook. I think my next poems about Lincolnshire will try to summon back the tastes which sustained its generations: perfect jam from Victoria plums, Sunday's dark rich 'chocolate mould', and the hot steamed sponge of 'Aunt Margaret's Pudding'...

Memoir

My mother cycled to the base
to teach. In the ploughed fields' place
green bunkers rose, a dead man's face.

'They had the rocket up today,'
my mother said, in the bright way
of her own pupils. She could buy

the NAAFI's doughnuts, shower our plates
with juicy sugar, walls of sweet
white ash. She never lost the weight.

Our kitchen dreamed American dreams,
forgot its mangle. From a van
came second-hand twin-tub's rattling sheen.

But you, inside the wired gates
where the Alsatians leapt at bay,
camp guard's son, counted higher stakes.

We listened to the washer's purr.
Kerouac passed you in a blur
from your friends' kitchens. It was Thor,

the missile made with nuclear tip
which rose from earth like a beached ship,
until Kruschev turned back his ships.

Your email tears my world apart.
Sleepless, I count my launching heart.
Three, two, one, zero. Now I start.

What?

It was a bus. It was the war.
It backed into the Brayford Pool
whose swans would drift towards the edge
like sparrows to a window ledge,
black at the heart of Lincoln. Or,
you have the story wrong, you fool,

it simply was your parents' fear
of what might happen, without lights.
Whether you skirt the reservoir
or eye the Severn's mud-slicked shore,
if, for one breath, you veer too near,
the wheels will swerve into the night.

It was the mailcoach, red as fox.
The panicked horses would not halt.
It was the wagon's freshest team
gone, overloaded, down the stream.
It was the cart with the best ox.
It was the bloody Romans' fault.

The Methodists

I knew the girls on climbing frames
who sang like cagebirds all break long
their Chapel anniversary song.

Its patterned bricks had birthdays too
with gales of singing, tea and treats.
The Chapel choir had doled-out sweets

to the contempt of us in Church,
quavering, glazed, in cheerless pews.
But England's gods stayed upper-class

despite the wild notes one girl dropped.
The Methodists told her not to sing
old, wicked songs. And so she stopped.

But at their fête in fitful sun
I heard their farmhand preacher, plain
in suit, thank God, then pray for rain.

He did not know the tide would turn.
The Methodists hated gambling, bars.
Our Sunday morning worships cars.

The cream walls close into a house.
A glum Prince, his thin girl, will rule
whose Chapel guards a private school.

Now in my waste land, freedom, I
can sing the wild black songs again.
For the fourth week, we have no rain.

Skies

It began, like wonder, back there
in the village's dark huddle
which I can never visit, like a star.

In high orbit, warm muddle,
my father's hard-packed arms, I passed.
Winter wind stilled, hedge and puddle

pure ice. Above my wreath of breath,
the weak eye of the one streetlight
beyond Back Lane and Temple Garth,

skies pricked with white until the night
swam with its stars. In their grave blaze
they filled my gaze like wings in flight

which never left, unlike the house,
the anxious moves, my mother's care.
For years I stood by my own house

with books and charts. My father there
could only name the tilted Plough
he followed with the snorting pair.

But I found Pegasus, the slow
sweep of the Swan, a fierce red eye,
the Bull. I watched the Hunter go

with frost's belt, over towns where I
now lived, where, still, the galaxy
boiled by his sword in clouding sky.

The books are laid aside. I see
new roofs, more weak lamps. Whirled and free
the stars, my calm dead, walk with me.

*In 'Temple Garth', 'Temple' refers to the Knight Templars, who
once controlled part of the village's land. 'Garth', a Viking word,
is used here of a farmyard.*

Playground

Children, you lined up for your game,
one tall boy called, 'Sheep, sheep, come home.
The wolf has gone to Derbyshire.
He won't come back for seven years.'
You raced across the wind-blurred ground.
But he was wolf. He plunged, he pounced.
Each child, when he clutched coat or cuff,
straight-haired, scuff-toed, became the wolf.

Are you a wolf, grey, slender? Yet
as, elegantly, you stroll through
the café's buzz, the city's dome,
what is it you do not forget?
How even then they lied to you?
Still they sing out, 'Sheep, sheep, come home.'

*We played this game in a Lincolnshire village school in the
1950s. In the 1980s, my mother, who still taught at the school,
told me that the children had replaced the old games with games
based on TV characters.*

The Price

Seven lives a year
were what the Trent would take.
A farmer with a lamb
he thought would never make

the grass and heat of spring
ducked through the hedge's hole
dropped down that fading bleat
to save a human soul.

Still, as my father grew,
sixpence or silver three'penny
was flung in once a year
to pay the Trent her fee.

Old lazy flood, great snake,
for all I say or think,
my purse lies near my heart.
Here is my silver. Drink.

Ditches

Still they lie deep, though I have gone,
the great dykes with their glinting load,
brown winter floods, fields' wasteful run,
planted too soon. Are there machines
which rear and dip from the firm road,
scoop glistening banks, clear rotted leaves?

Yet still, I know, there is a day —
a stone-blocked pipe, a tumbled tree —
when a man slides down with a spade,
beats back dead nettles, elders' switch,
sunk from the sky as under sea,
digs, sweats and clears the gurgling ditch.

As we drove down the empty road,
swept round the only bend for miles
my father drowned the lorry's noise,
told me a ditcher, working well,
sliced the dyke's wall, unhomed a rat
which squealed and bit him as it fell.

He caught the fever they called 'Weels'
(though now I know the name is 'Weil's').
The ambulance flashed past the drowned fields,
too late. For to this day, a man
can die from rats, as in the floods
of Bangladesh or Vietnam.

Then, by the only bend for miles,
smooth lawn flowed round a bungalow.
The farm's young shipwrecked wife filled hours
gardening bikini-ed. Calm and rich
this sunlit girl — the story goes —
sent several drivers in the ditch.

Lincoln OS 121

I buy this map for my Italian friend
Who in her hand-hemmed skirts at the war's end
Lived here; longs to go back.

Her Romans built the knife-straight major road,
Not that which wandered villages, I drove.
Here are their names. Go back.

Hemswell and Harpswell, Blyborough, Patchett's Cliff —
That limestone ridge we laboured up, whose rift
Sang water under land,

The spring's thin pulse beside the thrush's stone
A scoop of yellow shell, song's bubble gone,
Out of the noon's flat land.

Vast fields were sprayed by planes. The people kept
Their kindness, but grew sad before they slept,
Lincolnshire's curse, black blood.

Though skies bloomed, they blew higher in the Fens.
The cod's salt coast lay out of sight, land's end,
Laws, votes, remote, slowed blood.

Will Elena find high lanes choked by cars
The swede field crammed with houses, strange as Mars?
Will she mourn going back?

What makes or breaks us rides us to the end:
I murmur, like the spring, each name I send,
Brigg, Riby, Horkstow Grange, my long-lost friend,
I never shall go back.

The House

It was the house of childhood, the house of the dark wood,
four-square and safe. It was the second house
at least, to bear its name. The first was burnt: was charred
foundations, hidden by a timber yard.

I knew this in my dream: the house was same
and solid. All its yews, church trees, were strong
red wood of generations. As we came
out in the dusk sight heaved, house, orchard, gone.
Cold in the trembling grass we shivered there.
On open hillside, to the first stars' stare

I watched dark, unsurprised. I could remember
the bombers roaring low above the trees
to reach their high drome, though the war was done.
The house had strained and crumbled.
                    There is only
        the old magic, forced out in new ways.
Hard through the dream's cold spring I raised
My house again. My bones and my heart ache
In every joist. The altered rooms are filled
With lovely light: the only house
Which kills in falling, which you must rebuild —

        In new wood boxes, apples there
All winter breathe out sweetness, in cold air.

*This poem is based on the isolated Lincolnshire house where my
family lived until I was eight. It was a Victorian farmhouse,
called 'The Mount', which belonged to the rich farmer for whom
my father worked as a lorry driver. We lived in one-third of it,
and could not afford to heat the biggest front room, with its
marble fireplace. So this became a storeroom for crates of
Bramley apples, picked by my father from the old orchard.*

Robert Etty

In a piece on autobiography, Laurie Lee wrote of an urge to say 'I was here; I saw it too'. This sort of feeling, which is possibly quite common, has been one of my reasons for writing poems. I have written for some years about aspects of Lincolnshire, which may well be because its landscapes are my mental backdrop. Of course, I mean the long horizons, Tennyson's 'circle of the hills', the colours and shapes of fields and trees, the clouds building high on each other, and the birds and animals that share the county's skies and land.

And so my poems have visual elements. However, fragments of narratives are also important to me. Red-tiled villages and towns, clusters of new-builds, lanes, tracks, farms and churchyards recall and create people living their stories. They exist in real and imagined pasts and presents, and make their ways into what I write. Incidents find characters to act them out: someone indistinctly remembered from childhood borrows a name and plays a part in a place he or she may never have known.

My Lincolnshire poems are often set in the country, or on the edge of it, and their subjects tend to be uncelebrated events in people's homes and workplaces. One of the recurring figures is Raymond, who has no precise identity, but is probably drawn from family members and neighbours I came into contact with when I was a boy. He lives differently now, but the chimney poking above overgrown elders on any back road could be his. The sight of someone like Raymond on his plot underneath his sky might prompt me to write, and I change my mind on whether there is something romantic about him.

I was intrigued by a handwritten display card I saw once in a bookshop in Sussex. It was pinned above a selection of books by a respected poet who lived in the town, and it pointed out that, while *local poet* might be almost a pejorative term, the titles below were the work of a local poet with a national reputation — and that, anyway, every poet is local to somewhere, however wide the appeal of the writing. Probably it is true, though, that home ground is a central factor for some writers. Perhaps Lincolnshire underpins all of my poems, even when it does not appear in them. I cannot remember which writer it was who said in an interview, 'You can only write what you write'. It threw me when I first read it, but the sense of it has grown on me since.

Raymond's Mornings

Often he doesn't bother with bed,
but sleeps in his chair until four or soon after.
He stands at the sink swigging sugared tea,
looking out of the window as dawn brightens
through the high sycamores next to the church
and the first blackbird calls from the roof of his barn.
If a rat trots across to pick bird-table scatterings,
he opens the window without a click,
pokes out the tip of his rifle
and shoots it between its nose and its ear.
One morning last week he watched robins square up.
He tells it as if it were all of life.

Time for Raymond

He takes time on. It comes to terms with him.
He knows it better than he used to, how
it tells through clocks its monotone untruths
about when everything begins and ends.
The inlaid clock his mother left not ticking
on its clock-shaped shadow on her parlour wall
chimes down his hollow hallway any hour
except the right one. Certain cars, his postman,
waving people strolling past with dogs
can plot a day, so that his brisket's in,
he's pegged out shirts and gone to the bank
or to sleep in his chair not early, but not too late.
In the order of things, things lose their order
while clocks watch Raymond, in his own good time.

Bindweed on the Skegness Road

Occasionally a motorbike draws alongside
on the road to Skegness on a hot summer Friday
and roars at your car's open window. Your thoughts
have been pleasing themselves for a while,
but the afternoon has other ideas.
When it screams off ahead past the caravans
you breathe out, ease down and check your mirrors.

Sometimes it isn't a motorbike that's
biding its time in your blind spot. It and you
haven't kept in touch, but haven't lost
contact either. It's something outlived,
inapplicable, on a hard drive you prised out
and smashed with a hammer. *What's passed isn't past*
is part of the point it's driving home

as it passes you, and *Don't expect, but expect*
all the same. And how sometimes events overtake
what's happening, which means that what's
happening's not quick enough to reach the end
it has in its sights, or to reach it late
and miss the finish, or even to reach it at all.
None of this has a lot to do

with the trumpets of bindweed white in the hedges,
but it might cross your mind between Partney
and Gunby, which isn't the road you intended
to take, and you might not have, but for
a motorbike and associations
you couldn't pin down, and then for wanting to
and not, both more or less side by side.

Nikolaus Pevsner's Other Book

Reused Roman stone in nave and chancel,
Pevsner writes, and much of south aisle rebuilt
1886. Chancel arches wide
and Early English. Fine sedilia.
Font (octagonal, ornate) shows flowers,
and angels underneath, two missing noses.
Outside restoration's overdone, he thinks,
as if atonement for the sins of sun and frost:

no fooling such a searching eye about
how much a block of stone can hide. Inside,
too, he traces lowered floors, works out
where doorways led and wonders whether
hollow-chamfered transverse arches were
the wisest choice. Clee, Claxby, Claxby
Pluckacre, and Claypole, Claythorpe, Cleethorpes,
Legbourne, Legsby, Lincoln's long perambulations:

Lincolnshire's North Sea-aired naves, chancels, transepts,
pointed-trefoiled tomb-recesses, stiff-leaf knobs
and quadripartite vaults are noted down, with
halls and clock towers, schools and railway stations
part-way from antiquity to where we
are (or were when he stopped noting down).
It seems no stone or gold or wood's left out, but,
like the scallop worn from every chancel step,

the spaces everywhere define themselves:
the gap, for instance, in the holly hedge
along St Faith's south boundary, that Dick trimmed
as a shortcut from his bonfire patch to climb
the tower and wind the clock, and toll the bell
for funerals — the gap four muddy-trousered
bearers humped his coffin through that Friday
someone else was found to toll the bell;

the places under slabs the cars park on
that aconites turned yellow every spring,
and that damp cavern in the yews they sawed
the roof off so the lovers lost their nest
and ghosts kids said were chained up there flew out.
Pevsner lists leaved capitals and two brass plates
from 1430-odd, but couldn't
have a clue that what was also worth a note

was who threw Psalters from the battlements
while Mrs Steed was hoovering the mats;
why John Ward Wood, whose tombstone's cock-eyed
in the sandy soil the rabbits dig and pile,
was laid one August day to rest right on
the far side by himself; the Manor window where
the lads took trembling turns to gape in
when Mad Mavis took her skirts off by the fire.

It's not to say he *should* have had: that would
be another book, dust covered, copyrighted,
with a glossary of terms to clarify
how each step forward paved a way, or
blocked it, for the next (though most things ended up
the best for someone — and the ones things
ended worse for learned to live with it), but
that's no gazetteer. Here's Clixby (part-restored).

The Dog Days, the Dog Days

Heber stepped out of the shade in his brown cap and waistcoat
prodding a stick at some bullocks that we couldn't see for the hedge
until two by three and four they stumbled over the crumbly mud
and their hooves clocked slipperily on the grey tarmac.
"Coom on an' 'elp me leäd 'em yon, sither!" he called above them,
so we ran across and stretched our arms out and slapped the bullocks'
black and white haunches and hustled them up the dazzling green lane,
while Heber strode achily up to the gate and bumped it open
over the grass, and the bullocks shunted each other
into the air-raid shelter field. Heber was anxious and red in the cheeks
and the sweat smelt sharp in his unbuttoned shirt
as he fingered some sixpences into our hands.

And one afternoon we found big Bruce Cresswell (whose mum
drove a Mini and dad a Rover and lived in a two-chimneyed house
on the High Street) sprawling on the top of the shelter, smoking.
Blue flies were settling on the hot concrete and swivelling
and rubbing their legs. Bruce stubbed his cigarette out on a frog
and it scorched with no sound, but I hear it now.

A Lincolnshire Whirlwind, 1936

Most of them were there — Dad, Grandad, Grandmother,
the harvest workers — in the oak tree field,
but all with eyes down haymaking, and such
a baking sun, so no one saw it till
it struck. It whipped some drying heaps up in the air
and funnelled them across Bill Dashford's
milking shed and pasture to the lock
and dropped them there. Grandad hitched the rully
and they raked a full load up. Dad said
Grandad said the bloody next would take him, too.
It did, of course, and came back for the rest.

A Man with Six Bags on the Road
Looking Briefly Unsure of Where He Is

He's a man you'd expect to be wise
to this hedgeless road's illusion of bending
gently towards the coast, when really
it's only a practised feint on its southbound course
between fields where red tractors are ploughing in
stubble we've hardly had time to get used to yet.
Some of the roads play these tricks in the flatlands,
seeming hell-bent on what's up ahead
while keeping their tendencies under wraps
till we've followed too far to turn back.
Perhaps he's lost track of his sense of direction:
perhaps it's the road that's his destination
and not the undisclosed end of it —
he read Kerouac by the beam of a torch
and supertramps' autobiographies,
and walked out one midsummer morning
with just a jew's-harp and some lemon puff biscuits
to find a groovier life than the one
he'd had nothing to draw a comparison with.
Or is he more like the man at the flap
of the tent in the yellowing hawthorns
whose laundry and cover the breeze is blowing? —
whose unrepayable mortgage repayments
lay at the root of that midsummer lunchtime,
the van and the Westminster Chiming doorbell,
those men with diplomas in moving sofas
who blocked the pavement with sofas they'd moved
and an unpaid-for plasma TV.
When no driver knows what's round the corner,
it's tempting improvidence leering at someone
with wristfuls of bags to whom landmarks appear as
they do to us, but appear it a little later.
So the man says (in an indirect way)

when I park in a gateway and hold out some silver:
Don't give it me, sir is how he puts it,
taking a route to the west of my car.
Sand Skier, 12 to 1, Market Rasen —
and wasn't the rainbow a sight for sore eyes?
The double-decker to Bourne swishes past
on a timetable that it's learnt by rote
and he calls *Bon voyage!* from among his bags
and *Be sure you know you've got there, when you have.*

Joel Stickley

I was appointed Lincolnshire Poet Laureate in 2011 as part of the county's contribution to the Cultural Olympiad. As a result, I sought out, initiated or otherwise stumbled into many fascinating and unusual commissions, including collaborations with guerilla knitters, stained glass artists and composers, and was given the opportunity to do readings everywhere from air traffic control towers and music festivals to local radio and national television. Most enjoyably, though, I had an excuse to talk to people about poetry. I visited schools, libraries, social clubs, horticultural societies and all sorts of community events in order to do readings and offer people help in writing their own poetry. What I discovered was a county full of hidden talent, full of secret scribbling and literary ambition — full of poetry.

Theddlethorpe

At Theddlethorpe, the sea goes out for miles
and England falls away beneath your feet
while concrete bunkers hidden on the dunes
wait silently for rabbits to retreat.
Amongst the drift of wood and broken shells,
the path along the seaweed tide is lined
with white-on-red official signs that warn
that there'll be no reward for things you find.

He searches anyway, his school shoes wet,
imagination full of guns and gold.
He scuffs his feet through suspect spots of sand;
somewhere, back home, his dinner's getting cold.
He wants a souvenir of something real;
he wants to hold a thing that heroes held —
a hand grenade, an unexploded bomb.
He wants his heart to swell as theirs have swelled.

One scuffing school shoe thunks on something hard.
He kneels down and starts to excavate.
He feels it — metal, buried in the sand.
One hand digs deep, then pulls. He feels the weight.
It shucks off sand, emerges with a schwup;
the cavity refills with rising silt.
His breathing quick, he wipes the metal clean.
His heart swells now — excitement, fear and guilt.

He holds it up, the surface oddly slick;
it feels so heavy, alien and dead.
Then something from a video game he played:
'War never changes,' whispers in his head.
'It never does,' the lump of metal says.
He drops it, stung. It thumps into the sand.
A second passes — he is still alive.
It stares at him. He wipes dirt from his hand.

It speaks again — a hollow metal voice:
'But you don't know the smell of blood, my lad.
Your Xbox zombies never taught you that —
that churning in your gut you've never had.'
He turns and runs — the rabbits scatter out.
The puddled sands reflect the afternoon,
then rise to fill his footsteps as he goes.
The concrete bunkers stare out from the dune.

He stumbles on a sunken pile of kelp,
turns with his ankle, spins and sprints away.
Behind him sits the lump of metal, still;
he knows that there'll be no reward today.
He feels a burning in his throat and lungs.
Imagined spitfires cover his retreat.
At Theddlethorpe, the sea goes out for miles
and England falls away beneath his feet.

Thousands of Moving Parts

Written for the Museum of Lincolnshire Life
steam engine restoration workshop

'You've got to keep them working, or they'll seize up,' he says,
pulling on his his boots as he heads for the door.
His wife just smiles. 'Oh, is that what it is?'
There's a box of rivets on their living room floor.

The route to the workshop takes him through town,
past pubs where the people are just getting going.
He hefts his toolbox and keeps his head down.
What his evening holds, they've got no way of knowing.

There's a blow-down valve that's been giving him gyp,
a crack in the gauge glass that needs some attention.
The ash-pan's secured with a large bulldog clip
and the pistons have too many problems to mention.

But you should have seen it six months ago —
they're just rusting hulks when they first arrive.
It's tricky and fiddly and painfully slow,
but something he does to them makes them alive.

He arrives at the workshop and takes off his coat,
greets the machine with a pat and a smile.
He opens his toolbox and mumbles by rote —
'Hammer, spanner, pliers, file.'

This place is a shrine to making things work —
It's stacked to the timbers with half-fixed machines.
Enormous contraptions hide deep in the murk
at the back of the warehouse, like shadows from dreams.

In the puddle of light from a hundred watt lamp,
he settles to detail work, squinting his eyes.
The small metal clink as he tightens a clamp
echoes from engine to engine, then dies.

The hours burn up like coal in a grate,
till his hands smell of metal and his back starts to hurt.
When he finally locks up, he knows it's got late.
He's exhausted but happy, with oil on his shirt.

As he walks slowly home, the city's alive —
a thousand nights out are now in full swing.
Tomorrow, a new rusting hulk will arrive.
As the steam rushes through him, his heart starts to sing.

Veterans

Written for the Museum of Lincolnshire Life
steam engine restoration workshop

They come creaking back,
cracks in the paintwork and misaligned gears.
After years of faithful service overseas,
these are the veterans of peacetime.
There are crease-lines in fields in Brazil
that still have the shape these lads laid down.
Each blade found soil that would quickly yield —
some corner of a foreign field
that is forever Boston.
Lost in the march of globalisation,
they were stationed in places too far from home,
where they alone remembered enough to be proud.
Howden. Tuxford. Clayton & Shuttleworth.
The names must have seemed strange
in the South American sun.

They still run, some of them.
And the sum of them is more than their worn-down parts.
They have iron hearts, these old soldiers.
They have iron hearts and ash-filled lungs.
When they were young, they turned the earth itself
and wealth was generated somewhere in that firebox.
The knocks and bruises were badges of pride,
but inside, something was rusting.
They were trusting, as a soldier often is,
and this — this is their reward.
A sword changes fewer lives than a ploughshare,
but now they're finding there's something they lack.
So back to birth the metal comes
and one by one the veterans —
they come creaking back.

St. George's, Goltho

At Goltho, a ploughed field bulges —
divulges its secrets one pottery shard at a time.
There was a village here.
Then, for six hundred years, just a church.
The new bell lurches in the wind,
headstones lean in at strange angles —
a tangle of brambles and branches and epitaphs.
"THE COMING OF THE LORD DRAWETH NIGH."
The sky reaches down and smooths the edges of the bricks.
1446 was a bad year.
But, back before the crops failed,
there was a village here.

This poem, along with several others, was written for the Churches Conservation Trust's Archway project; the poems were incorporated into new window designs by stained glass artist Derek Hunt and installed in the churches which inspired them — this one in August 2012. The tiny church of St George, Goltho was subsequently gutted by fire, in October 2013, after a lightning strike.

The Normal Parade

Written for the 2012 Lincolnshire County Show

Everybody's got debts, but Susanna's in deep —
her negative equity's losing her sleep
and she drives an old Daewoo but dreams of a Jeep,
so at weekends she takes risks to prove that life's cheap;
puts on goggles and lycra then climbs up and leaps
from a high-dive to water that's six inches deep.
The adrenaline rush gives her something to keep
when her mortgage repayments are looking too steep,
so she walks in the normal parade.

Andy makes notes on the interviewees —
just an endless procession of kids with degrees
who go so far to show off their own expertise
and the life skills they learned when they "lived overseas"
that they sound like they suffer from brainwash disease.
How he longs to get home, give his missus a squeeze,
then go down to the garden where nobody sees
and relax with a drink and the beard of bees
that he wears for the normal parade.

Mr Khan quit his job to become his own boss
but the shop that he opened now runs at a loss
and his dream, like his shop sign, is losing its gloss;
so he closes up early and then goes across
to the pub near his house where the jukebox plays Bros
and he sneaks to the toilet and then starts to toss
off his clothes and get changed and he knows it's pop dross
but he bursts from that toilet and he is Matt Goss
as he walks in the normal parade.

As Andy, Susanna and Mr Khan know,
life can move along fast when the hours pass slow
until all of a sudden you've nothing to show
for those years of work except debts that you owe —
be they money or time or ambition and so
it's important to have something hidden below,
something small and defiant that makes your heart glow
and this idiosyncrasy helps you to go
and walk tall in the normal parade.

If you write your own episodes of Dr Who,
play Stravinsky and Beethoven on the kazoo,
construct life-sized giraffes using only bamboo,
live for weeks on Pot Noodles and tiramisu,
have a massive collection of foreign shampoo
or a box full of gum it took years to chew
or a hobby or passion or something you do
for the pure joy of knowing it's only for you,
come and walk in the normal parade.

Kathryn Daszkiewicz

'To live in the Fens is to receive strong doses of reality. The great flat monotony of reality; the wide empty space of reality...How do you surmount reality, children? How do you acquire, in a flat country, the tonic of elevated feelings?'

Graham Swift, *Waterland*

I suppose I regard Lincolnshire through the lens of an outsider, although, as I come to write this, I realize that I've lived here longer than anywhere else. I ended up in the county because of a chain of circumstances — as opposed to a conscious decision to relocate here. But I have stayed. The Fens fascinate me — and particularly the idea of them before they were drained, when they were vast and eerie and man seemed an alien species in a land of birds and fish. I did a lot of research into that watery era before I wrote the sequence *Fenland Bride*, at one point spending a whole day at Ayscoughfee Hall Museum before it had been refurbished, and reading and scrutinising everything that was there.

Lincolnshire means big and beautiful skies and, of course, flatness. When a friend took me to visit the site of the Gilbertine Priory at Sempringham where Gwenllian, the last Welsh princess, was brought as an infant and incarcerated as a nun, it was these features which formed the backdrop of the poems I wrote imagining her experience. Someone told me about an actual condition called *fen sickness*, which afflicts non-natives who are used to hill country. The idea took hold, especially as my own relationship with the landscape was somewhat unresolved.

Until I came to the county, I'd never seen barn owls regularly and watching their white shapes floating above the hedges in the early morning was a highlight of the thirty mile commute from Spalding to Grantham which I did for several years along the back roads past Bourne Woods and Grimsthorpe Castle. It's also the place where I've seen the most kingfishers — both at Denton Reservoir and along the Grantham canal, often in the least scenic parts. And birds have a habit of flitting through my work in some form or another.

Funnily enough, I was named after Katherine Swynford (the heroine of Anya Seyton's famous novel with which my mother was very taken) and she is buried in Lincoln Cathedral, so I had a link with the county even before I set foot here. That was in the late 80s — although I had driven through it endless times on the A1. Living now in Grantham — the only Lincolnshire station on the East Coast railway — I like to think I have the best of both worlds: access to London in just over an hour, but roots, of a sort, in a place that has maintained much of its character and wide open spaces.

from **Fenland Bride**

i. Against the gold

I picture your heart as a map of the Fens:
neat compartments circumscribed
by straitened rivers, artificial cuts;

I haunt the fringes only. Sometimes
I drive and drive just to escape.
The roads are flanked by dykes

so deep an injured biker
lay out of view for days. Here
there is no room for manoeuvre.

As I head for Crowland, fields
gang up on me, uniform as graph paper;
even the flash of a tulip field neat

as soldiers on parade. I yearn for
the randomness of poppies shaking
their heads blood-wild against the gold.

ii. Behind the wheel

Often — on my trips to anywhere — I'd be
slowed by tractors, their huge wheels

spinning out mile after arduous mile
as their exaggerated treads

spewed a detritus of straw,
dead confetti floating on the wake

of diesel fumes. I was always the one —
leading a train of frustrated motorists —

who was scared to pull out — even
when the road ahead was clear.

iv. Tulip parade

Red tulips signify a love which burns
  after the decapitations heads by the million
with hearts so black to show how passion chars
  are pinned to floats in decorative ways
Ferhad a Persian youth adored a maid
  paraded to the cheers of day-trippers
called Shirin. When she shunned him Ferhad fled
  coachloads clogging the arteries
into the desert, fallow as his hopes
  of this small town. Tamed blooms
his tears sprang to life as tulipan
  they will never throw off
named after tulbends Turks wind round their heads
  their pursed-lip primness
they slowly stretch exposing all their pain
  to let their petals yawn
contorting into acrobatic shapes
  in poses of wanton abandon
return to bulbs from which they'll rise again

v. Gull

Out of the corner of my eye
a gull spells freedom
in this sky of skies. Tricked
into acrobatics by vastness
it loops and gyres without
the safety net of the sea.

Used to the regal glide of ships
it fails to gauge the speed
of the white van. Falls jagged
from the air. I feel the day
contract. There's no telltale brown
of a young bird on its feathers —
it was old enough to know better.

It lies now on the tarmac.
The nearest waves are the brown,
static furrows of a ploughed field:
a place where crows rule.

viii. Sour milk

I am not one for reading tea-leaves
but an owl ghosts across the surface
of my coffee on a day when you are out
again. No one has done the shopping.

By daylight the heart that is her face
will fade as ashes in a dying fire.
But at night, over the fens, on silent wings
she will rise, pale as ivory, from the ruins

she makes her home, the buff of her back
dusted with cinder grey. I crush the note
I'm left and push away the cup.
I do not have to drink.

Behind High Walls:
Gwenllian at Sempringham

i. Moons

It's whispered Gilbert's mother, growing round,
dreamt that the full moon slid down from the sky
and settled in her lap. It was, she said, a sign

the child in her belly would wax great. He did.
His painted halo's luminous as the moon
that gapes across these fens on a clear night.

My own months are not measured by the moon.
That flood is stopped. Another gift
unused. My mother died in giving light to me...

My family is dispersed across this land -
caged princes, chastened sisters - all to stanch
the blood that might be spilt should we be free.

So I gaze at the moon I am allowed — an English moon
over these endless fens. Here it will never snag
on the jagged crowns of hills.

ii. Captive

I ate an oyster once. Unlocked it
from its shell. There was no pearl

inside its grey and slippery heart
no moon on a grey night caught

between the clouds. I have read
the gospel of St Matthew where he tells

about a pearl so special
a merchant sold

his everything to own it.
I see my story in an oyster shell:

pearl of great price
that never saw the light.

iii. Sunset on the Fens

is stained glass freed
from lead. The colours

kiss and marry, bleed
into new unions —

pink as the limbs of cherubim
or gold as angel halos.

Sometimes the clouds
are edged with silver

like the drawn sword
of a warrior saint. And

when the year is old
copper and flaming orange

vie to set the sky alight.
This is not hell; but something

in my bones tells me
never to call it home.

iv. Clouds

Carmel, Sinai, Gaash, Gareb,
Ephraim, Gilead, Hermon, Seir...
These are names I give the clouds —
but only when I deem them grand enough.

Mountains I've never seen. I'd like to think
that on the journey eastwards I was soothed
by the sing-song undulations of the hills,

rocked by a wordless lullaby
that rose and fell until earth
lost its joy to the judder
of hoof on stark, flat ground.

There's none to tell me tales
(the kind that merge with memory)
about my infant self. But I know
that Wales boasts hills - and mountains too.
And I miss them — somewhere they are in my blood.
I do not know their names.

v. Memorial

The ripple of a wimple
is quite plain
side-on in upright stone
fresh-hewn
from Penmaenmawr
unchiselled.

The head's bowed
like a nun
who is at prayer,
asking perhaps
that she might,
in her lifetime, know
the rise and fall of hills,
of her own tongue.

As she once did,
it stares across the fens
a land oppressed by skies
sometimes so leaden
that she could not bear the weight.

Kingfisher on the Witham

Three sullen steps
ahead you saw him first.

And though you deigned
to give a branch by branch

account of where he hid
I couldn't get my eye in

till he moved, low willow
to low willow. Later I

thought even you
could never dim

the flare of him
that swift, bright nib

rewriting patterns
in my winter head.

He flew, his breast
the colour of desire

but perching, turned
and ice extinguished fire.

Rory Waterman

I was born in Belfast, and my first home was in Coleraine, County Derry. When I was two, my mother, who had grown up in the small North Kesteven village of Dunston, left my father in Northern Ireland, and moved with me to the house where her mother, my aunt and my cousin lived: a cramped but beautiful Victorian stone lodge house a mile from Dunston and slightly closer to the even smaller village of Nocton. I was not permitted to visit Ireland, where my father still lived, until I was ten — though the legal conflict over custody and access rumbled on into my primary school years, and as a young child I remained disoriented by a sense that, in some way I couldn't quite define, I belonged elsewhere.

Ireland became a sort of unreachable imagined paradise to me. Lincolnshire, on the other hand, was where growing up *did* happen: slowly making friends; learning to flatten my vowels just as mum, at her convent school, had learned not to; going to a terrible comprehensive school in an over-grown village where my English teacher couldn't spell 'Wednesday', bunking off it most Wednesdays and other days indiscriminately, and flunking my GCSEs; taking a girl down a bridle path with nothing but vanishing into three-foot-high meadow grass on our minds and walking back out again too soon; getting pissed for the first time under a railway bridge with one of my best mates (who still lives up the road), and playing tennis on a knackered, ex-RAF tennis court until it was too dark to see. Most of this involved a small integral aspect of dreaming of elsewheres and what I'd do when I found them. I rarely if ever intended to read a poem then, let alone write some of these things into poems.

I grew up a little bit, and left at twenty, destined for the slightly brighter lights of Leicester. Then I lived for a while in Durham, then briefly New England, then for six years Bristol. And I have somehow found myself, at thirty-three, settling (for now?) in Nottingham, about twenty miles from the county border. This was not by design, let me tell you, but I am glad nearly to be back in the county which I understand more intuitively than anywhere else, and where so many of the people I care about still live. Something in me still changes for the better every time I head 'home' — each time I catch that first glimpse of Lincoln Minster, tiny on the ridge fifteen or more miles away, from somewhere near Brant Broughton. The people who live there are luckier than most of them realise. But I won't be moving back to join them.

Epicentres

St Denys' is making its stab for the Maker
and the 07:19 for Lincoln is rattling through its break
in the fields, then over a culvert, and on it you sit,
and look up from *Bizarre* straight through the view

where a church spire is flat on the whiteness of sky
with one dour gull shooting clear across its tip
and over the rain-bright roofs, cracked tarmac, then you,
and on to the coast where sharp groynes cut the breakers.

53° 09′33.17″ N, 0° 25′33.18″ W

A lodge-house to an estate, once: the front wall
still ends with one redundant brick gatepost,
its rustic latch clicking only to wind,
and the clean bulk of its limestone cap
shorn of clogs of English ivy, carious and precarious.

There used to be a long metal water-butt
out of bounds, snug to a wall, pungent
with moss and webs, its content a black
lilting mirror when I'd raise the lid
that was wooden and rotten and gave slightly.

And there was a low-slung roof on a breezeblock annexe
with a fat windowsill and convenient external piping
that occasionally broke and had to be mended;
and a cigar-box of old green pennies and shards of pot
from the garden, out of sight in a cracked soffit.

But the side gate remains, a wrought iron cross-hatch
mass-produced in a distant foundry, showing
bends for the feet that are no longer mine,
that kicked off and made it a shrill, dull swing;
and the fence is the matt-green my grandmother painted,
though tarnished now, and in places peeling.

Access Visit

Your afternoon pint; my Britvic pineapple juice;
a bag of prawn cocktail gaping in the middle.
The lounge at the Wig & Mitre was Daddy's choice.
And then, at six, my taxi home; a cuddle
before I left you waving at the corner,
bound for my mother, our monthly weekend over.
And she would always seem a little warmer
than when I'd left, and I'd be slightly colder.

How could I know what an alcoholic was?
The Wig & Mitre's now Widow Cullen's Well.
The snugs have been pulled out, the walls made bare;
but the place still has the same sweet, musty smell,
and I'm going in for a drink again because
I know I'll find a part of us in there.

Over the Heath

The truck grinds by
and pumps out grit;
the road glints and
goes still.

The barn owl that
had not finished here
returns. But with
its fill

of scavenges,
face ruffled in mulch,
the vole is lost
and safe

so the silent spectre
flits away, its
moon face to
the moon

and rears unknown
against a copse,
claws tipped for
the strafe

and something dies
too soon.

He filled her between
the hay-bails in
that Dutch barn, now
abandoned,

where the wind
catches its breath
in the stanchions,
air-gun holes.

Then they sprang up
light and lightsome
and she tugged his hand
with her hand

as the breeze pulled
at the poppy-heads
and rabbits shrank
round boles.

But how soon he'd
grow indifferent
as the tick she
couldn't see

that was part of
her for longer
than he would choose
to be.

Out to the Fen

Suddenly, the shattered hedges, ancient culverts,
our huge ruined villages, give way as
dimpled fields tilt to the Fen
and the treeless otherworld begins.

A farmer churns a vast parched field to a desert of stalks
in acres of dust and haze. Blueflies thrum
unperturbed, by a verdant ditch straight
as a Midwestern state highway, vanishing both ways

into hardly a ridge: a slope that stretches
and loops for hundreds of miles to the same sea.
Along its lip, behind dykes, the low farms and
hardened cottages stare across the flats.

It's like a coast, but what might be sea
is a sea of outstretched meadows, fresh green wheat
nodding like so many donkeys,
dotted with clumps of poppies,

and the elders have flowered. We snip
the heads by dusk, in a silence of ditch noise
and birdsong, for cordial and fritters,
sometime later, then scatter

hares in the headlamps, and thud through clouds
of skitting gnats as distant lights
blink to let us know buildings are
over there, people are over there, and now

it's time to go.

Pulling Over to Inspect a Pillbox with a North American Tourist

It lists beneath a sycamore   .
swashing in high summer leaf,
and takes a hit from underneath:
a root-knuckle bulges along the floor.

Its eight loopholes have fissures, sprouting
thistles; through each the wheat is fattening.
"What's this thing *for*?" A starling sings
its wind-up song. The sun slides out.

And this taste of piss, that Fetherlite
slumped in the corner, those Holsten cans,
the markered slogan FUCK YoU! ✎ S. DAN
do not try to answer. Might.

William Bedford

I don't think we chose our obsessions. They choose us. I was born in a damp terraced house in Grantham in 1943, but throughout childhood I loved visiting the farm in South Lincolnshire where my father grew up. Pillar Box Farm was in Kirkby Green, and the rich family history I inherited is the theme of many of my poems, including most of *The Fen Dancing*, published in 2014.

My father was in the police, and when I was nine he was transferred to Cleethorpes, where we lived just behind the promenade until 1959. We arrived just in time for the 1953 floods, the tide flooding the street outside our house. For several years, during the summer holidays, I worked on the fairgrounds on the promenade, and briefly as a barrow boy on the fish docks when I left school. My first novel, *Happiland,* is largely about those years.

In 1959 my father was again transferred, this time to Hemswell in North Lincolnshire, his rural beat including several villages and USAF Hemswell where the Americans had the Thor Intermediate Nuclear Rockets. That was where I began writing, introduced by American friends to the great American poets, dramatists and novelists of that time — Lowell, Berryman, Ginsberg, Mailer, Bellow, Kerouac, Arthur Miller, Tennessee Williams. I worked on a chicken battery farm before studying shorthand and typing at a local college, hoping to become a journalist like Hemingway, but under relentless pressure from my father, signed up for the police cadets. In 1963, after a nervous collapse, I left Lincolnshire to work in the City. I wrote about these years in my second novel, *All Shook Up*.

Over the years, I returned to live in different parts of the county. For a while, I rented an isolated cottage on a tulip farm in South Lincolnshire. I lived for some years in North East Lincolnshire, in the Wolds, in landscapes where many of the poems in a forthcoming collection, *The Dancers of Colbek*, are set. Figures often associated with different parts of the county — Tennyson, Clare, Lawrence, Wesley — are in several of my latest poems. Many of the short stories in *None of the Cadillacs Was Pink* are set in the northern parts of the county, and on the coast.

Though I have lived for many years in London, Sheffield and now spend much of my time in Oxford, Lincolnshire haunts my writing. I do believe in roots. Wherever I am, the strange isolated landscapes of my early years colour my imagination, as images and metaphors and symbols, and as the source of endless stories. When I look at old photographs from the nineteenth century of members of my family on the farm in Kirkby Green, it is almost as if they are looking back at me, urging me to tell their stories.

Pillar Box Farm

They called it Pillar Box Farm
because it was a farm and had a pillar box.
Had to be, really, when you think about it.
The postman didn't know when the pillar box
was fixed in the wall. 1840s he reckoned,
when the post began. Before his time anyway.
I might have guessed that without being told
just by looking at the old photographs.
But he was joking. Passing the time.

In the photographs, a horse crops grass.
There is a reek of stack yard and silage
rising from the cold celluloid.
Chickens peck at the verges.
I can see my grandmother's strong arms,
the smoke from grandfather's pipe.
A sheep dog watches us from the hedge
in case I try to walk into the picture.
The gold lettering on the carrier cart
says *John Bedford: farmer*.
My family name etched into timeless sunlight.

The Journey

i.m. Charlotte Annie Bodsworth
Grantham: 1944

The long road from the farm was longer then,
the chickens fed, breakfast on the table,
then stopping trains and unfamiliar stations
to Grantham's cobbled market squares.

You came to see your newborn grandchild,
the poet sleeping in his earliest days.
Nothing would have stopped you, a right lass,
livelier than the youngsters in your black shawl.

You died weeks later, as the bluebells came.
'Seeing you,' my father said, a family joke.
The long journey a likelier story.
And mine, in after-years, struggling for words.

You came to see your newborn grandchild,
a day's trip away from Pillar Box Farm,
to make your claim on an unknown future,
plant the seeds of our secret harvest.

Then

for Alison Brackenbury
North Lincolnshire: 1959–1963

I had to kill them when it was time to go,
take my leave and catch the stopping train.
Rhode Island Reds they were,
kept for the eggs and kitchen table.
We tarred the wounds of the flock's victim,
locked the hutch at night with twined wire.
If we left the gate open, two followed us
up the garden. One dared the kitchen,
sitting for a photograph on my shoulder.
The other stayed in the yard outside.
I had to kill them when it was time to leave.
The one sitting on my knee was the tamest,
used to pecking seed from warm hands.
She seemed surprised, finding no seed,
not worrying I was going to break her neck.
My father had to fetch the farmer. I cried.
All twelve were gone in a heaven's blink,
a grubby fiver, then biscuits and a cup of tea.
We sold them for the table. Our own stood empty.
Too poor a food for us in pheasant season.

The Fen Dancing

Kirkby Green: 1914

The sheep washing was our spring surprise
the old farrier says,
showing us round the village:
summat lively for the youngsters,
and the old uns if they'd a mind to admit ...
I stretch my mind to listen,
stories I can only hear in words:
a horde of children skreeking to the beck,
young women twisting aprons
through gnarled fingers,
horses shrouded by a gadder of flies.

That's a mite fancy for us he shies.
I might leave fancying for my own memories.
We're strangers here,
though grandfather farmed the sixty acres,
a two-horse farm and sheep and pigs for the table.
We walk on, *nowt left to say.*
In Baumber's Field, the muntjac deer listen,
wary of the uninvited strangers,
alert to winter's crizzling grind.

Who is listening?
I might fumble to imagine:
the boy scaring crows in Baumber's Field ...
the lovers wrapped
in spring hay swaddling ...
ghosts, knowing what the fields know.
But the shepherds are all adrift,
their flocks in locked pens
waiting, bleating,
their collies threshing the stockless fields ...
and the women are all adrift,
asking who will go in 1914,
some to live, some to die, as the grass yields ...
and the villagers are all adrift,
calculating loss from a cumulus of clouds,
the geese, telegraphing their loud prophecies ...

You got that right, he says without shying.
And afterwards?
There will be an evening of dancing,
where you cannot tell the fen from the dance,
or the dance from the wild fen dancing ...
the brawl of cold water in the beck
chiming to the chapel bells ...
forget-me-not flowers
drowning in the wash of lovers' feet ...
But who's speaking
I cannot say,
the farrier or something forgotten,
as the crows circling over Baumber's Field ...
as they always will, they always will.

The Father's Tales

In the loft above the barn
you heard the Irish labourers chanting spells,
black magic rituals the dour Wesleyans feared.
You did not recognise the words:

Hail Mary full of grace
whispering like the pebbles in the beck,
bringing shadows of unknown stars
back to earth. You had your own fears.

Your ghosts were unseen familiars,
the heroes of apple-scrumping wars
shimmering in the orchards of a room,
companions of your grandfather's slow dying.

You were sent to listen to his tales:
the men who fought at Waterloo,
friends of the years before school
fen-dancing warmth into the darkened room.

Elizabeth wouldn't be mithered to listen:
The minister from the chapel visits every day,
round about teatime.
He knows the Word, never hears a word you say.

Now mourning swallows the farm.
You took the bright farthing for crow-scaring.
Hid when the minister chanted psalms.
Didn't hear what the psalmists had to say.

The Potato Gatherers

for my father

The potato gatherers were the ones,
Van Gogh faces in a Van Gogh barn,
where they slept upstairs after work,
or rested when they weren't working.
'They're counting the harvest,'
your sister reckoned. 'Or maybe praying.'
You thought they were witches,
chanting to fetch curses from the dark.

The Methodist minister said the same:
'Decent folk don't pray on their knees,
or out of doors, like cattle.'
From Manchester himself,
he often talked of cattle,
as though the farmers in the pews
would understand his parables better
if he used the language of herds.

The hens got mithered either way,
squawking at whoever stole their eggs
for the field workers' breakfasts.
In a lane, you found a string of beads
and took them to the minister.
He said they were a curse
that would bring famine and pestilence,
panic among the young women.

Nothing much happened.
The potato gatherers went home
when the potato harvest was finished.
The minister was driven away by an aunt
who said she'd seen all this before,
he wasn't a man made for loneliness.
The blacksmith put a new lock on the barn,
and the fields sank back into silence.

You walked with your sister to chapel,
harvest supper and then a dance.
You didn't care for dancing. In a corner,
you ran the string of beads
between your fingers,
and they chattered like pebbles in the beck,
or the crows when you went crow-scaring,
humming a music nobody recognised.

The Ford

for my grandfather, John Bedford

The pony-and-trap has stopped in the ford,
my father sitting on my grandfather's knee,
sunlight glittering off the cold water.
At least, it looks like cold water. The horse drinks.
They are half-way across, caught by a shout
or one of those summer fleetings,
a whisper of bees you take for a thought.
They might be going to Sleaford market,
or down the stream's banks to collect berries.
Nobody knows who the photographer is.
My grandmother's sister, the gossips said —
Annie Bodsworth who hanged herself —
but that might just be mischief, probably was.
Her cheeks were still warm when they found her,
in the old barn, close by the stack yard,
the herd waiting in the dark to be milked.
There was a hare sitting under the rope,
looking for magic, according to my grandmother.
My father recalled she had blue eyes,
'The bluest eyes you've ever seen',
and a voice 'the sweetest in the village,'
those high notes in the Methodist chapel
distracting all the men from the preacher.

But that was more than seven years later,
when he was ten. He is three in this photo.
His father is holding him closely,
in case he falls into the fast-flooding ford.
And the photographer might be any woman,
the village women warm for my grandfather,
because he played accordion on Saturday nights,
and would walk a girl home so they said,
before saying a friendly goodnight,
though nobody believed that. Wasn't likely:
a kiss beneath a harvest moon
wasn't a thing you'd miss out on lightly.
And he was a talker, and a dancer too,
when he wasn't playing the accordion.
Women would have liked that.
He couldn't remember who took the photograph,
but the pony's name was Penny Farthing,
named after a girl he knew called Charlotte
who rode round the village on her bike,
laughing because she had perfect balance.
'Nobody likes to forget things,' he told me,
staring into the shallow ford waters,
hearing a girl's laugh. 'Nobody reckons on that.'
He gave me his favourite bone-handled knife,
which I lost digging for frogspawn in the river.

David Cooke

I moved to Grimsby in 1983. Like many things in life it was quite by chance. As a young man with a family to support, I had my eye on promotion and applied for the post of Head of Modern Languages in a large comprehensive school in Cleethorpes. At the time, I must have impressed myself by bagging the first promotion to have come my way. However, it didn't take long as a 'middle manager' to appreciate the near impossibility of attracting decent staff to what has always been an out of the way part of the country. I don't think when I applied that I had much idea myself of where exactly Grimsby or Cleethorpes were, or knew anything much about them. These days they are designated the 'unitary authority' of North East Lincolnshire, but back then were a part of South Humberside, the poor relation of North Humberside across the estuary, all of which was a bone of contention amongst the 'Yellowbellies' who would have no truck with 'Yorkies'. Still, coming as I did from an Irish family, there was something very familiar about such tribal loyalty and the discontents engendered by an arbitrary line on a map.

Looking back three decades, I never imagined that years later I would still be living here. Nevertheless, in spite of the demands of work and the increasing impossibility of moving on, as property prices elsewhere soared, I wouldn't want to paint too gloomy a picture. With a modest salary you can live well here. Moreover, soon after my arrival something strange happened. I started to write poetry again. Strange? Well, yes, because for much of the 1970s I had written and published poetry. I had even managed, by some fluke, to wangle an Eric Gregory Award in 1977, but then, almost immediately, the poetry dwindled away. I can only speculate as to why it started again.

However, it must have helped that at the time there was a thriving poetry scene in Grimsby and this was something new to me. At university I had written in complete isolation — hard to imagine now with the proliferation of workshops and creative writing courses. In those Humberside days the county council sponsored a literary journal called *Proof*. My next door neighbour, William Bedford, was a well published novelist, poet and critic who had a long-standing association with *Agenda*, as did Robert Richardson, the editor of *Big Little Poems*. Shortly after I arrived Peter Bennett, that marvellous poet, did a year's residency and edited *Grimsby Roads*, an anthology for local writers. Across the water, in Hull, John Osborne was achieving great things with *Bête Noire*. Then, by another fluke, my first collection, *Brueghel's Dancers*, was published by Freeman's Press in Boston. However inept its contents appear to me now, it was nonetheless a book, which meant that in some way I must have 'made it' as a poet, which I might well not have in different circumstances.

At Woody's Top

Trying to see it, I look across a landscape
on the raised edge of Lincolnshire,
whose flat productive acres have wrinkled
into the rise and the dip
of the Wolds, as if geology
had assumed a rhythm like verse.

And though it's all a question
of pressure and upheavals,
and the slow relentless stroke of weather,
my gaze settles on a view
that has the fixity
and composure of a final draft.

Beyond the mizzling bluster
of a late October morning
the distances are sealed in silence,
where gulls flicker above the copse
like random thoughts
that may or may not amount to something.

The Manor House at Alford

Finding his feet on the right side of history,
some notable, a name, acquired this house,
when he laid new money down for impeccable
brickwork and the chamfered beams

upholding its fireplace, the ceilings,
a world; and blithely assuming
what may have seemed the burdens
of stewardship, his life was well appointed.

From dawn till dusk, and by degree,
days creaked on cogs and wheels like the lift
in which his wife ascended. Hutched in the attic,
his servants' lives were entangled in bells.

While their descendants, freer now
and more uncertain, can pay to view
the relics of each sanitized era,
glimpsing here through perspex

the insides of walls whose handsomeness
was all a fascia, a blind, across
an arcane structure whose ties could not hold.
Slowly the house disassembled itself,

becoming a sump for wealth
in deferential twilight, as lost trades
and the skills of mechanicals
were reinvented to claim back a premium.

And if we're now unsure who owns it,
trustees are tasked to make it pay its way —
its garden reduced to raggedy box,
a few late windfalls, pecked at, abandoned.

Ships

Drummed in by the Brothers
with medieval efficiency,
I had always known since schooldays
that *navis, navis,* feminine, *ship*
was how we got to *nave,*
its pews aligned in shipshape rows,
its congregation, facing east,
like pilgrims on a voyage
toward the promised land.

And on that Open Day
in the parishes of the Wolds,
when they unlock the abandoned
churches, I climbed the ladder
into a belfry that might
have been the inside
of an ancient sailing ship,
its timbers held together
without a visible nail,
its bell wedged and silent.

Like a fool or a sinner
who has set out on a westering
journey I looked across low hills
that heaved, collapsed,
and petered out, their green
swell disappearing
beneath unruffled sky.

Ontology

On Cleethorpes beach the tide is out,
where gulls dispute their stretch
of puddled sand: a paradigm to taunt me
as they snatch what gain they can,
their broken cries a colloquy
that's tough and unforgiving,
while against each blast that freights them
I hug my collar closer. Optimism —
It's like a string of toytown lights,
painted bulbs that vie
with the elements' big effects.

The Owls of Cleethorpes

i.m. Nelson Mandela

No one knows how long the owls
had spent inside the trees,
reviled at first and then trapped
by the god of grudges.
Hooped in rings of growth,
a drizzle of sap sustained them
through the creaking dark.

When strangers came
with bags of tools they set to
and lopped the branches,
silencing their canopies.

They made each trunk
a pedestal, chiselling free
the birds until, larger
than life and monumental,
they shook off at last
their wooden feathers.

Beyond the Humber

for Ian Parks

An immeasurable distance seethes:
ultima thule a blank frontier
where grey sky and grey sea
boil down to a blur of extinction.

You could wait forever here
for sirens' voices cheeping
a sugary southern song —
so no need now to block my ears
against the lilt of danger.

The heroes here were workaday:
trawlermen and whalers,
their mythology composed
of sweat and casual deaths,
hard graft on keel-roads.

Brought to this coast by chance,
I, too, must learn to live here now:
my collar turned to a wind
from the edge of the world.

Freeman Street

Location! Location! Location! It's a mantra
the upwardly mobile intone,
who have set up shop elsewhere —
catchpenny merchants with tricks up sleeves,
purveyors of pleasures and deals.

On a street where ripples of boom
and bust have long since subsided
beneath the tide of failure
the footfall of 'three day millionaires'
kept all the rest in business.

Awaiting turns to land their catches,
trawlers rode at anchor, backed up
beyond the docks. Their crews staggering
ashore to re-establish land legs
lost them again in pubs

where men now washed up at forty
nurse disconsolate pints;
while workless youths hang out,
honing their skills with cues
in a room above the Scope shop.

Marks and Sparks pulled out, leaving
a space filled by Mad Harry's
discount store that held its own for a while,
until it went the way
of Tony's Textiles, the *Polski Sklep*.

Along this windy channel
nothing much survives beyond its lower
reaches, where Asda's thrives like a final
outpost. There's a place that fixes hoovers;
an Alpha course that fixes souls.

From time to time — like a twinge
of conscience — there's talk
of schemes, regeneration: but who throws
good money after bad? *Everything Must Go!*
the sign says, when it's already gone.

The Grimsby Chums

They are swaggering down
Freeman Street, comrades in arms —
their steps buoyant with self-esteem
and a changed sense
of where they are from.

At their backs Icelandic bluster
has chivvied them along
from the dock end's rough banter
— its lacklustre backdrop
of estuarial grey —

toward Top Town's flags and brass.
Easy going veterans
of drink-fuelled brawl,
they'll sign up and knuckle down —
disciplined recruits.

And after endless nights
on far-flung fishing grounds
how hard can it be
to march in style
across some fields of beet

beneath vast sky
that seems familiar —
like the girls lining up
for any lad with a bob or two
and a lopsided grin?

Clare Best

When I became Writer in Residence at Woodlands Organic Farm, near Boston, in 2005, I had been to Lincolnshire only twice and I scarcely knew The Wash from The Bay of Biscay. Four years later, by the time *Treasure Ground* was published (it was my first collection, and all the poems were born of the area around Woodlands), the Lincolnshire Fens had become one of the primary topographies of my imaginative life.

Although my work there extended over almost three years, I was never at Woodlands for more than four days at a time. My home, main job and family were all in Sussex, and I could only manage the residency by leading a quick-paced double life, shuttling between Lewes and the Fens, sometimes by car, sometimes by train.

Throughout those years, I was always trying to catch up with myself, which made my experience of the Fens fiercely intense. When I was at Woodlands, I was very busy running community projects and I had to steal the time to walk with my notebook. I would dream and remember the poems into being as I travelled back to my Sussex life. At times it felt as though I had left my head in the South Downs, at times as though I was unable to retrieve my heart from the Fens. Soon I realised that I could only write the one place when I was in the other, and that the displacement itself was integral to my love affair with Lincolnshire.

There is another aspect of my relationship with Lincolnshire that I want to mention. At the time of my residency, I was contemplating and taking the decision to go ahead with preventive double mastectomy. I had the surgery in December 2006 and returned to Woodlands in January 2007 to continue my work there. My feel for the landscape and my writing about it are inextricably linked with this period of enormous change in my life. 'Self-portrait without Breasts' — the poem cycle that came out of that set of experiences, published in *Excisions* in 2011 — has many connections with the Fens.

Woodlands Farm is dear to me as the place I was first accepted as a working poet. I was there to facilitate writing, to help people reconnect with the sources of their food and with the landscapes that sustained them. I was also there to write myself. I felt privileged on both counts and I shall always be grateful for the residency and for the encounters with people and places.

And those landscapes themselves will forever feed my imagination. The famous limpid light, huge skies and unforgiving winds; the liminal spaces of sea-wall, dyke and marsh; the soil's wealth, the courage and industry of those cultivating the area; the rich bird life; the smells of samphire and brassica and salty mud — all these and other elements of Lincolnshire have shaped my thinking and my writing and my thinking about writing.

To the Fens

The Peterborough-Spalding rail link over the fens. March, frozen feet, I stand by an open window as the train rattles east over black sea-ground, heading away from the sun-setting west into blue and purple, towards the windy edge of the Wash.

This time of day distorts perception. Lines of trees are whiskered onto a bowl of sky like rare mould growth. Jet trails over the horizon are fragmenting, silver as silverfish. The evening's violet cloud banks are phantom hills to me: I come from the south, where to look down from above is to see half my county from a chalk ridge. But here a railway embankment gives enough perspective to look out across fields swimming shade and last light. Here is almost underwater, almost tidal.

Criss-crossing dykes and cutting over plough, we're just above sea level, above soil level, and it's as though we're trying to take off on a long runway into night. Red-brick villages with dark slate roofs huddle either side of the railway line. They seem to be inhabited only by yellow lights and satellite dishes.

This is bulb country with polytunnels striped over vast prairies, and as the train shudders onwards the stripes flicker away into serial vanishing points. By May, when I'll next make this journey, potato plants will show on the ridges between trenches, alternating black and green, black and green, soil and leaf.

God's dripping pan, they call this place. Put anything on or in the ground here and it tends to grow, and fast. It reaches down, takes root, makes the most of the mysterious dark earth and the picked-clean skies. Everything grows. Crops. Hedgerows. Weeds — willow weed, persicaria, dog daisy, camomile, creeping thistle, bindweed, fat hen, and the rest.

I can almost believe the houses here began as sheds that grew and grew, putting down roots, digging in.

heads expanding

stretching their skins
mud-cushioned
bedded with nettles
and soft remains

squat and bald
leafy   half-hidden
or out in the open
like something dropped

each to be scalped
scoop-hollowed
each to have cuts
for eyes   nose   mouth

all to hold fire

Listening to Lincoln Red

for Bruce

They puff and bellow, a chorus
for the wind in the metal roof

keeping time with their feet,
trampling the straw, no let-up

between the rub and rattle
of iron feed bar; gush and pour

of piss; soft drop of cowpat
hitting the floor. Lean in

for the steady rhythm
of jaws moving — slow, soothing.

Hear the snorts, exchange of air:
in-breath, out-breath, humid

moan and vibration of barn.

Afternoon, March

The shadow of the Dutch barn
reaches over Struggs Hill;
blades of winter wheat
cut up through winter mud.

Barn-shade darkens the ground
towards a knuckled hedge.
Beyond — light, distance,
field creased against field,

unfolding flat as a map
to the farm's margin
where containers roll across the fen
dubbing the sound of low tide at the turn.

How to be Considerate to Sheep

When you're known to the sheep you meet,
put them at ease. Don't grimace or frown.

Provided they can see, sheep read expressions
just like you and me. Regular shearing

keeps fleece away from eyes. Horns
should not be allowed to grow too long.

Sheep perceive negative and positive emotion
so hang pictures of cheery faces

on the walls of the shearing shed or barn,
reassuring images for them to focus on.

These social animals will be less stressed
if the slaughterman's a stranger

than if it's someone they know. Please
encourage the unknown slaughterman to smile.

Treasure Ground

Silt Pits, Tunnards, Bloodsworth, Goatmans,
Pinchbeck, Fosdyke, Trumpet Hall.

Names raised like bog oaks from the fen,
briny as North Sea gales. Marsh-wet names

for deeping, dredging. Names to whisper;
names to carol. Names to harrow, seed or plough.

Hawthorns, Wigtoft, Struggs Hill, Mandyke,
Seas End, Holbeach, Algarkirk.

Names cursed and kissed down generations —
flooded, drained, reclaimed, converted.

Gull Field, Chittle Lane, Pyewipe, Frampton,
Lammings, Daughtons, Treasure Ground.

Airman

Flying Officer Ray Bédard, aged 25, of 439 Squadron RCAF, was flying from RAF North Luffenham in a Canadair Sabre MK2 on 23 June, 1953. He broke from formation and was killed after bailing out while his aircraft was in a steep dive. The plane crashed in a field by Whitehouse Farm near Woodlands.

There's still the geometry
of lanes and dykes and hedges,
a spirit-level horizon. East, the North Sea
sheet-metal smooth to the sun.
West, a thousand fields beyond Long Tankins

hundreds of nameless shades of green.
Now, as then, the invisible skylark
rehearses, rehearses. The marsh harrier
glides low over wheat, drops on a vole.
Hares lie in hollows, unblinking.

Edgeland

Between marsh and fen, creatures don't respect time and space. They cross and re-cross boundaries. Walk here and you'll surprise more and more of them, putting up pheasant from the fields, heron from the ditches. Meadow pipits dive and swither over stubble. Hare and rabbit scatter to the hedges. An owl might burst from the upper window of a small red-brick barn and ghost over new plough, looking for a daytime kill.

It's just twenty minutes walk, past giant manure heaps and a water pumping station to the new sea wall. Climb up through a gap in the tangled hedge of black and red berried thorn. Walk along the top: it's as though you're patrolling the divide — marsh with muddy creeks and low tide on one side, on the other side, fen, reclaimed land. This man-made ridge is the watershed between wilderness and cultivation.

November. There's still a warm wind. If you drop down from the wall you'll see how it combs the hummocks of near-horizontal grass, rippling the brackish water in the creeks. A few weeks and winter will be here, viscous salt water all but freezing as it laps at the silky mud.

Curlew skim the marsh, their wings catching sea light. They drive in fours and fives, blades carving air. Their cries banish all others. Their long, curved beaks will penetrate eight inches into mud for lugworms, and if they run out of lugworms, they come inland for earthworms.

Things aren't fixed in this edgeland. No-one and nothing will be here long. The fen lies at least ten feet lower than the marsh and one day the sea will return. Soon, perhaps. Brazen on a spring morning, high waves breaking over the wall. Or at night, seeping in under cover of darkness. One way or another she will be back to reclaim what's hers.

Michael Blackburn

If there is a single word to describe how I find Lincolnshire it is *congenial*. Congenial in its earliest sense of sympathetic and connected with kindred. That's even though when I arrived here I had not visited before or had any family associations with the place. I suppose most people have the experience of visiting somewhere and feeling quite at home for no obvious reason. That's what I mean by congenial. I felt at home in Lincolnshire as soon as I came here more than a quarter of a century ago. It was not so much a homecoming as an arriving at home for the first time.

Most of that is to do with the landscape. Lincolnshire is big, it has big skies and a large amount of flat land (though the county is not totally flat, as outsiders always think). But it has a pleasing and subtle variety combined with a great sense of privacy. There is a certain hardness in its light, a purity and sharpness that enables you to see great distances on clear days. This combination of distance and space makes demands both physical and metaphysical on its inhabitants. It engenders an impulse to measure and calibrate and to step beyond. It's no surprise to me, then, that the county has produced both seafaring explorers (John Smith, Matthew Flinders, John Franklin) but also mathematical geniuses like Newton and Boole.

It's a county that was once fuller of people than it is now. Its immense history is often no more than mounds in the earth. You can be surrounded by this history of work, worship, politics, commerce and conflict yet be quite alone, hearing only the wind or birds or a barking dog or a passing car. You sense that something great has been and gone, yet nothing vital has been lost but continues in a new form. The American philosopher, George Santayana, sums up this sentiment for me when he says, 'Everything in its ruin [...] seems in England to live a new life: and it is only this second life [...] that is English.'

And that, for me, is very congenial.

The Lost Villages of Lincolnshire

The lost villages of Lincolnshire
stow their broken frames underground,
so low your level sight will overlook them
to find a further field or wood or sky.

Only when you take a higher view
from a slope or wold will you see
the smooth ditch and ridge of their bonework,
the shallow shadows they make in green,

then remark as you pass how this land lies
untended, left to nettles and sheep,
a farmer's waste, fenced in between
fields of rape or flax or wheat;

discernibly dark still after centuries
the footpaths leading through and out
made clear in posted pathways that join
headland walks and wide green lanes;

bodies, like buildings, all brought low
in a soft rumpling of soil, poisoned
with poverty or plague or simply being
too far from a road for survival;

their couplings and dyings, their daily prayers,
their counting of coins and cutting of bread,
blood, breath and bone, all the same now
to the rising lark and the falling rain.

Water Kingdom

We pushed it back, squeezed its flow,
dug ditches, dykes and drains,

the Forty-Foots, the Twenty-Foots;
piled up the black earth to keep it contained,

said, *come in Cornelius*, to the Dutchman
who measured the levels and dried them out.

We alchemised this liquid world
to something we could walk upon

but still it keeps on coming back,
falling from heaven and bloating the becks.

Drive between villages and you'll see it now:
wide fields water-slain, silvered with new lakes.

Woodpigeons Come Home to Roost

woodpigeons come home to roost
and kestrels come to the wood
rabbits feed on the open field
and in the green strip along the road
their eyes in headlights dead as moons

Over the City

over the city, the pool, the railway
the falcon keeps his height
spooking the pigeons that turn
and turn again between him
and the rooftops, dropping down
where I cannot see them
till they rise again, grey on grey
to left or right and him always above
patient, unhurried
ready as a switch

Surveillance of Landscape

surveillance of landscape
no landscape is innocent
regulation is necessary hence
the colour coordination of crops
mind how that field of wheat
oversteps its boundaries
escape is illegitimate
there will be legislation
already there are too many acres
infected with poppies
too much red

Tractor Music

tractor music
lapwings and marsh harriers

for a moment all I can hear
is the wind through these trees
thud of an apple falling

rooks in the stubble
scavengers on a battlefield

in the complete circle of sight
the sky behind everything

After Ice

after ice
water
then ice again
wrecking the cheap tarmac
over so many months
like here where I turn
right descending from the top road
to the lower
the cathedral on its hill
in the distance
whichever road I take

I Like That Sound

crow in a big tree
I like that sound, he said
and that as well
tiny plane high up

bird scarer off behind
and I like that sound, I said
and the wind in the trees

and so it continued
as we cycled along the lanes

Sam Gardiner

I was born in Northern Ireland and lived there until I pursued an architectural career in London, where I spent seven asthmatic years before taking refuge on the Lincolnshire coast, attracted by its breath-giving sea air and affordable housing. On my first visit to Cleethorpes I watched an elderly couple searching the sands for pieces of coal washed down from the mines along the River Humber, which is detailed in my poem 'Sea Coal'. During the next forty years I lived in Lincolnshire and worked at my poetry as never before.

Apart from brief periods in the town of Louth and the historic but trendy city of Lincoln, where the war tank was invented in 1916, I have always lived close to the sea and continue to enjoy frequent excursions into rural Lincolnshire, which is inexhaustible in its interest and is a large landscape still spacious enough to absorb the increasing numbers of visitors and refugees from urban England. I consider myself fortunate to live among such varied and friendly communities, and to have found a wife here.

Sea Coal

Down first thing for a breakfast of air
by the sea where far off oilskinned
figures dig for lugworms, while here
a long black tidemark defines
the sea's jurisdiction on land.
An old couple, long winter coats
thrumming in the wind, trudge the line,
bent double for nuggets of coal
no bigger than Oxo cubes. Finally
in a plastic bag slaked with sand,
they have amassed a shovelful.
I hope they get their drudgery's worth:
a firelit hearth, perhaps: warm hands
at bedtime to touch each other with.

Just Churches

The insurance agent I had come to see
and the antique shop next door I hadn't
were closed for lunch. Even the chintzy café
was Closed for Lunch. A heavy drizzle, slightly
short of pattering, kept Barton on Humber
steeping, but St. Mary's was available and there
and so was I. She took me into that peace,
the laid-to-restfulness of entombed centuries,
which recoiled when a bolt of lightning hit
the sanctuary, backed up with a show-stopping
Oh, bugger! normally inaudible, at the altar.
A second flash. I had begun to pray that my
life insurance covered acts of God, when
a rotund Norman pillar was elbowed aside
by a burly prophet bearing a tripod, flashgun,
and pendulous with small black boxes.
Hello, I thought I was here on my own.
I didn't disturb you? he hoped,
and shuffled his equipment uncomfortably.
You see, I didn't really ought to be here.
I'm not into religion, just churches.
Old woodwork, joinery if you like,
from way back when carpenter was king.
I wished I'd thought of that, and turned to see
the door swing unlatched in the wind to admit
a grey ghosting of King Carpenter's descendants
sporting planks, and Burberrys and cameras.
Don't know much about Christ and that.
Carpenter wasn't he, from Galilee
or somewhere? Not from Grimsby like me.
I bet he would have liked this roof,
each beam and rafter from rugged oak.
The joints! The strength lies in the joints,
male and female, mortice and tenon,

tongue and groove, half lap, double cog.
I could go on, he broke off, eyes drawn
to the upturned, dark hull of the roof,
and frowned. *The trouble is*, he mused,
the best joints can't be seen from the floor.
He gestured aloft with a smart zoom lens,
noticed it and confided *Redundancy money*,
hitching his Pentax. *But just imagine*
those poor sods toiling away, only to leave
their personal best hidden away from sight
like so much rubbish. They were told
that God could see it, that's what mattered!
His laugh was loud enough to wake the dead
who caught and knocked it wall to wall
until it fell to dust. His *Great acoustics*
was barely a whisper. *We can't build*
like this anymore: all regulations,
British Standards, Codes of Practice,
all money, no honest craftsmanship.
He Englished his disgust into *My God,*
I need a pint. And then, *Anyway, it was nice*
to meet you, and remember, twinkling
like a chisel, *When and if you die,*
the first thing you'll need is a carpenter.
He turned and banged out, whistling like a lark
before it sees the dark shape hovering.

The Lincolnshire Stilt Walkers

'They that inhabit the fennish country [...] were in Saxon times
called Gyrvii, that is, Fen men or Fen dwellers. A kind of people
according to the nature of the place where they dwell, rude,
uncivil and envious to all others, whom they call Upland Men;
and who, stalking on high upon stilts, apply their minds to
grazing, fishing and fowling.'

William Camden, *Britannia* (1586)

Hissed by geese and woldheads alike
and with stilts broken by the water,
they ripple across the blue ponds and patches of sky
they share with other waders, redshank
and curlew, or in their uncivil tongue 'pyewipe'.
From time to time they must look down
at their wavering selves minding their step,
sounding the bottom, and placing long wooden feet
on their faces, like breaking mirrors.
But when the ice crackles on blind pools
and clears like cataracts they must stop
and think themselves rich in sky and wetlands,
which are neither earth nor water but both,
and not mere gooseherds feathering their beds
while the wild geese overhead write a V, and N,
a W, and then a V again on the stormy sky.
Good spelling avoids the successful goose,
which can read the earth's instruments,
the sun's dials and map's co-ordinates
to within half a wingbeat of touchdown.

After a long day's work blocking drains,
breaching weirs and wrecking sluices
the stilt walkers or, more unkindly,
fen slodgers, invite the water back
to soften the land they lease from the mist
the ancestors left, and from which they keep an eye
on the greasy ganderers splashing home
to their fishwives and goosegirls, calling out
to one another and corrugating the fens with starlight.
Ignoring the morning's high cirrus,
cumulus clouds plump with rain boil up,
drench the wolds and leave them streaming,
and skim across the levels without slowing down.
They leave no trace of their passing, and take
their shadows with them. Fenlanders' prayers
are answered when the hillwalkers catch the rain.

To the aid of these malcontents the civil commotions
Came opportunely and were probably the means of
Continuing the race of stilt walkers for another century,
But when all the tracts of fen land were successfully
Drained and enclosed the race became extinct.
   'The law doth punish man and woman
   That steals the goose from off the common,
   But lets the greater felon loose
   That steals the common from the goose.'

No, not extinct. They are not, cannot, must not
be permitted not to exist, though such is their
historical shame that from Spalding to Woodhall Spa
they fight shy of using their stilts in public,
preferring to leave them propped up
under the stairs, oiled in readiness for the righting
of ancient wrongs by natural disasters. Meantime
their rude and uncivil natures are barely detectable
except at checkouts, in car parks
and when expected to prefer rather obvious
mountain scenery to the subtleties of the plain.
But the Gyrvii would have been better
written down at the time, and written better,
by a scriptorium of goose-pens to disappear
into books where we could read them,
than now being conjectured in Microsoft Word
because they vanished and left nothing behind,
although this, of course, was the idea.

In addition to Camden's Britannia, *this poem draws on Kelly's*
History, Gazetteer and Directory of Lincolnshire *(1856)*

Sky at 6.30 A.M.

Betty lives at her living room window
with a view of seventy-one other
windows, which spend their time
trying to make sense of one another.
A light is switched on and a curtain
is drawn, while the sky above
spends the day rearranging itself
in shapes and colours that make each
new day a huge festival of movement.
Clouds softly collide in rivers of air,
tumbling and rumpling into curls,
snarls and kisses, celebrating change,
primeval creatures, their passing expressions
reflecting life's disarray on earth.

No two of Lincolnshire's skies are ever
the same, they bring worlds of weather.
This cloudless dawn has dimmed its starlight
and left only the morning star
poised above and ready to drop into
the sun-rimmed bowl of half a moon,
crescent and star artistically arranged
to invite interpretations, and meanings.

But 6.30 in the morning belongs
to the paper girl. She brings newspapers
to half-asleep houses up smooth paths
through tilted lawns of wide-awake daisies.
Rushing, throwing her bike about,
running out of time, quick smile for Betty,
she has noticed the thin bright moon
between door and door, and knows what it means.
It means that perhaps she can make a wish,
or wish that her old one is answered soon.
She straightens her red school tie
and pedals off. Only six more to go.
           Five.   Four.

East Somercotes Nativity

Winter wetland, flat mud that never dries
except on tyres in the miniature bike shed,
on the tractor and trailer parked at the gate
and on the wheels of empty prams at the door.
Drive gently through our village, beware
of the five- and six-year olds wearing faces
of mythical horses, cows, donkeys and sheep,
faces that know more than can be said,
and now line up on stage with Jack Merry,
Alfie Gates, Mike and Abel Adamson, and
assorted wise men, shepherds and innkeepers.
Twenty shiny first-year fixed-wing angels,
including Daisy Hewitt and Sukie Polegate,
would like to fly back to the land they
came from but are short of lift and propulsion.
We fiddle with our wings in sympathy.

A mystified Joseph has forgotten his lines,
or remembers he was cast by God
in a non-speaking role, and stares blindly
at the spotlights, until the Virgin Mary stabs him
with a sharp little finger. The baby Jesus, pink,
plastic and complacent, is taunted by a newborn
in the audience until the only hat in the hall,
a matted trilby, smothers the heckler
and smuggles him out for a quick hugging.
Saved from Santa Wanta Lotsa the stable
animals and wise men in tea towel turbans
unite to send their carols down the centuries,
out across the Marsh between the wind farm
spinning and the seals quiet at Donna Nook.

A grainy winter darkness has gathered,
and a fresh East Somercotes breeze disperses
goodbyes and keeps the dew from freezing.
The little ones blow about and find parents
enough to take them home to tea and telly.
Daisy Hewitt carefully parcels up her wings.
She doesn't know when she'll need them again,
or how often those adult know-alls need wings
and can't remember where they left them.

Rennie Parker

As a poet, what matters to me most about Lincolnshire? I think it's the spiritual depth in the landscape and also its unexpectedness: medieval remains which you don't find anywhere else, isolated level crossings in the middle of nowhere, sudden festivals in tiny parish churches where there aren't any houses within sight — you don't have to look hard. The stuff comes flying at you, and when it has the right combination of artistic surprise, you have to write it down. I've also gathered a lot of material due to a previous job in community arts, where I was paid to travel around the county setting up workshops. Total heaven. I'm not Lincs-born but I've lived here longer than where I grew up, so I'd like to think I am naturalised by now. If I'm away for more than a week, I'm scrabbling at the hotel walls and counting the days until I can get home.

Candleshoe

The pollen was flying and the wind was out of its cage
I had negotiated a route of ancient cowpats

Even the lark could not go higher
Everything further away than I thought.

I heard crickets questioning in the grass
And dry yellow plants like struck matches

Gave me a hill of gold.
A mole had turned up the shining ear of a shell.

I was there on the earthstump looking at the grass
And a white feather travelled with me

As far as the fingerpost saying *Away*.
Behind me there were emptied barns

Proclaiming their innocent status,
The cows moved one to another

In their separate department.
Now I am head high in wild angelica and campion

Their scattered petals are beneath my feet.
Which one of you is my enemy?

Because I possess double fortune
Because I am Fool with my steeple hat

Creature of many directions
And my cathedral is limitless space.

I am she who embraces chaos —
My hand breaks through the spider's web

While sheep with their T-bar heads
Lie with the rook's feather undisturbed;

And when the sun walks over the rim
The standard thistle raises its violet lamp

Where Fool is, down in a roomful of grass.
I am there on the vacant manors

Rammed beneath the earth's parapet
Where tractors scale their lines —

Having no number I am everywhere
At the crossroads you'll see me vanish

At the point where needlebright damsel flies
Go practising their neon signs

And the insect shakes the bellflower
On the angled plains of Pelham's Land.

The Pilgrim Approaching from a
Different Road

Just as mine host was talking about the lightning-strike
a tractor waddled into view.
It was my 50th visit to heaven
still finding the whole place different.
Today the lines are more marked on the field itself
as though recent rain had defined them.

Five grey birds are turning like knives
in sudden unseasonal wind.

     It is Sunday —
only the farmers are out,
wobbling in their warm high cabs.
They are finding reasons to go somewhere,
farmers and the tearoom patron.
He carries his weight like a careful package.

'The bricks were raining down everywhere in the village,
plugs blown out of their sockets...'
The crusty groundwarp itself a cause of activity:
elbows ready to rise.

And I have six more miles before the clouds race in before
 the rain,
past the hieratic sugarbeet factory
in its armoury of brick and steel,
past the hardboiled smallholdings
clamped to the river's straight edge.

A chiffchaff is sharpening its whetstone.

'Disintergrated', the man said.
Where the thunderbolt struck it shattered
a metre of solid masonry and its concrete bed.

Butterwick Low

Alas, *girasole*
it is the wrong time of year for you.
Your torches are extinguished
in a line from Marjoram's Motors to Deeping St. Nicholas.
There is a place called Malice Farm,
there's another place called Tongue End
and the birds are pecking your eyes out
in the blackened stumps of January.

Meanwhile the turbines are lording it,
they cartwheel across the fen
slicing the wind to size —
and you are more forlorn than ever,
the chewed bristles of an old brush.

I am wishing you slow summers
under the pressing heat.
I am hoping to see your gargantuan heads
follow my car as it glints past
on the stagecoach route to Spalding.
But now you are the bent skewers after the barbecue,
what's left of the trashed cabinet.

Alas, *girasole*
the tractor is coming for you
and the road-salt gritter is worrying on
with hot stones rattling at its heels.

The Several Places at Kempley

Branches were out in the air
like nerves. We'd walked enough
to say this wasn't it,

we should have come round
by a different way. But here
is like my own domain

at Sempringham —
the zig-zag rutted track,
the priory all gone:

a risen hill, the church
a castled tower of light
where brilliant fingers of sun

smash at the panes.
There's two of them out here;
easy to mix them up

and wander off down there
where stubbed-out orchards line
the hogsback roads for miles

and ill-positioned houses
abut at sudden junctions.
Listen, the breathing woods

are closer now than death,
the lost travellers in time
reclaim their evicted land.

They found remains near here
At Postbox Field. Emergency tape
Rings the affected site,

The three kings, the shepherds,
the white police van crawls
across historic daffodil fields

to break the pleated lines
of fresh-tilled winter farmland.
The stark remembering thing.

Stopped

The landscape brims with giant sheds.
Private. No entry. Keep Out.
The grass stands up in alarm —
at the raw new fishing lake
men are set out like pegs.
Something is stretched too tight.

Have I gone wrong? Nothing
except the ticking of an electric fence.
This is the marked wood,
its deep green silence amazing.
I stop and follow the map
where nobody is displaced.
Then a car slows down behind me:
she wants to know why I'm here.

Suspicion follows me around,
the heron launches his spear
grouse beat upwards in panic
and farm dogs racket at the gates.
At the end of your private road
I'm guilty of being a passenger
in the human business of occurring.

Something Happens, Sometimes Here

From the open window plates clank into sinks.
Pampas grass, blue and sharp, thrusts a head.

Its rapiers wait, stiff with outrage
stuck in this dusty corner of rural Lincolnshire

home of lost causes and chimneypots.
A spindryer drones on down to a stuttering halt.

The River of Life Ministry proclaims God's kingdom
in faded handbills: *the wisdom of the wise is foolishness*

and: *Rottweiler puppy for sale, eight months old.*
A jet stripes its lonely line down the sky's big face.

It's Saturday, it's July, and nobody's out
the dance is cancelled, the caravans moved on

it's business as usual in silent towns
with window displays that haven't been changed

since the day the cinema was bombed in '44.
And junkyard houses march backwards

to green seas crested with kale, waterbutts, canes
the praiseworthy end of labours

and sheaves of Golden Rod. It's all in order, friends
your lives are pure there's nothing to reach you here

the kingdom is safe, the bunting flutters in peace
streaming from thick-legged architecture,

men will soon be home in their brylcreemed hair
your bakelite sets alive with plosive announcements...

I walk down a blind lane. Houses in curious brick,
tendrils escape from the sides of crumbling ledges

Grade 1 viola floats past. A piano goes stumbling after,
playlist to How I Began. And somebody comes.

Acknowledgments

William Bedford: 'Pillar Box Farm', 'The Fen Dancing', 'The Father's Tales' and 'The Potato Gatherers' are from *The Fen Dancing* (Red Squirrel Press, 2014). 'The Ford' is from in *Collecting Bottle Tops* (Poetry Salzburg, 2009). 'The Journey' won First Prize in the *London Magazine* International Poetry Competition 2014 and 'Then' won First Prize in the Roundel Poetry Competition 2014.

Clare Best: all poems are from *Treasure Ground* (HappenStance, 2009).

Michael Blackburn: 'The Lost Villages of Lincolnshire' is from *The Ascending Boy* (Flambard Press, 1999). 'After Ice' is from *Spyglass Over The Lagoon* (The Knives Forks And Spoons Press, 2011). 'Water Kingdom', 'Woodpigeons Come Home to Roost', 'Over The City', Surveillance of Landscape', 'Tractor Music' and 'I Like that Sound' are previously unpublished.

Alison Brackenbury: 'Memoir' and 'The Methodists' were first published in *Stand*. 'What?' was first published in *PN Review*. 'Skies' and 'The Price' were first published in *Scintilla*. 'Ditches' is from *Then* (Carcanet, 2013); 'Lincoln OS 121' is from *Singing in the Dark* (Carcanet, 2008); 'The House' is from *Selected Poems (Carcanet,* 1991). 'Playground' is previously unpublished.

David Cooke: 'At Woody's Top' was first published in *The Dock*. 'The Manor House at Alford' was first published in *New Walk*. 'Ontology' was first published in *The Undertow Review*. 'The Owls of Cleethorpes' was first published in *Poetry Salzburg Review*. 'Beyond the Humber' is from *In The Distance* (Night Publishing, 2011). 'Freeman Street' was first published in *Envoi*. 'The Grimsby Chums' was first published in *Agenda* in Winter 2014.

'At Woody's Top', 'The Manor House at Alford', 'Ontology' and 'The Owls of Cleethorpes' will be included in *A*

Murmuration (Two Rivers Press, 2015). 'Ships' is previously unpublished.

Kathryn Daszkiewicz: *Fenland Bride* was commissioned for the 2003 East Midlands 24 8 Project and is from *In the Dangerous Cloakroom* (Shoestring, 2006). 'Kingfisher on the Witham' was first published in *New Walk*. 'Behind High Walls: Gwenllian at Sempringham' is previously unpublished.

Robert Etty: 'Raymond's Mornings', 'Nikolaus Pevsner's Other Book', 'The Dog Days, the Dog Days', 'A Lincolnshire Whirlwind, 1936' and 'A Man with Six Bags on the Road Looking Briefly Unsure of Where He Is' are from *A Hook in the Milk Shed* (Shoestring, 2013). 'Time for Raymond' is from *Half a Field's Distance: New and Selected Poems* (Shoestring Press 2006). 'Bindweed on the Skegness Road' is previously unpublished.

Sam Gardiner: 'Sea Coal' and 'Just Churches' are from *Protestant Windows* (Lagan Press, 2000). 'The Lincolnshire Stilt Walkers' was first published in *Dream Catcher*. 'East Somercotes Nativity' was first published in *Lincolnshire Life*. 'Sky at 6.30 A.M.' is previously unpublished.

Rennie Parker: 'The Several Places at Kempley' is from *Secret Villages* (Flambard, 2001). 'Stopped' is from *Borderville* (Shoestring, 2011). The other poems are from *Candleshoe* (Shoestring, 2014).

Joel Stickley: 'Theddlethorpe' was featured on: *Country Tracks*, BBC One; *Breakfast Show*, BBC Radio Lincolnshire; *A Golden Thread*, Inspire Lincolnshire online video. 'Thousands of Moving Parts' and 'Veterans' appeared in *Stories of Steam & Oil*, exhibited at The Museum of Lincolnshire Life and hosted at lincstothepast.com. 'St George's, Goltho' was commissioned by The Churches Conservation Trust, and exhibited in St George's, Goltho. 'The Normal Parade' was featured on BBC Radio Lincolnshire and *A Golden Thread*.

Rory Waterman: 'Epicentres' was first published in *Archipelago*. 'Pulling Over to Inspect a Pillbox with a North American Tourist' was first published in *Poetry*. The other poems are from *Tonight the Summer's Over* (Carcanet, 2013).

Contributors

William Bedford grew up in various parts of Lincolnshire, and has lived in the county at times during his adulthood. He is an award-winning novelist, children's novelist, poet and short-story writer, his work appearing in *Critical Quarterly, Encounter, Essays in Criticism, The Independent Magazine, London Review of Books, The Nation, Poetry Review, The Tablet, The Washington Times* and elsewhere. He is on the Editorial Board of *Poetry Salzburg Review*. His novel *Happiland* was shortlisted for the *Guardian* Fiction Prize. His selected poems, *Collecting Bottle Tops*, and selected short stories and non-fiction, *None of the Cadillacs Was Pink*, were both published in 2009. His newest collection of poems is *The Fen Dancing* (2014).

Clare Best is a poet, writer and Creative Writing teacher and facilitator, with a background in fine bookbinding and publishing. She is an Associate Lecturer in Creative Writing for the Open University and Writer in Residence at the University of Brighton. *Treasure Ground* (HappenStance, 2009) resulted from a residency at Woodlands Organic Farm near Boston, in the Lincolnshire Fens. *Excisions* (Waterloo Press, 2011) was shortlisted for the Seamus Heaney Prize. Her prose memoir, *The Papermaker*, was shortlisted for the *Mslexia* Memoir Competition 2014. Her website is at: www.clarebest. co.uk

Michael Blackburn was born in north-east England and lives in Lincolnshire. A former editor on *Stand Magazine*, he founded Jackson's Arm Poetry Press and Sunk Island Publishing. He was the first Literature Development Worker in Lincolnshire, and in 1995 he was a Writer in Residence on the Internet. He has published a dozen collections of poetry, the first being *The Constitution of Things* (Northern House, 1984) and the latest *Said Marlow Suddenly* (OneHand Press, 2015). He became an FRSA in 1998 and his personal papers are housed in the Special Collections of the University Library at Leeds. For three years he was the Royal Literary Fund Fellow at the University of Lincoln, where he now teaches English and Creative Writing.

Alison Brackenbury was born in Lincolnshire, where she went to the village school at Willoughton and the girls' grammar school at Brigg. She now lives in Gloucestershire. She has published eight collections of poems. The most recent is *Then* (Carcanet, 2013). Her ninth collection is due from Carcanet in Spring 2016. Her poems (including some about Lincolnshire) can be heard online at the Poetry Archive http://www.poetryarchive.org/. New poems, and blog posts, can be found on her website: www.alisonbrackenbury.co.uk

David Cooke won an Eric Gregory Award in 1977 and has been widely published in the UK, Ireland and beyond. His most recent collection is *Work Horses* (Ward Wood Publishing, 2012). He has two collections forthcoming: *A Murmuration* (Two Rivers Press, 2015) and *After Hours* (Cultured Llama Press, 2017).

Kathryn Daszkiewicz was born in the north east of England but has lived and worked in Lincolnshire for over twenty years. She was awarded a writer's bursary by East Midlands Arts in 2001 and a selection of her work appeared in the 2001 Shoestring Press anthology of *New Writing* that same year. *In the Dangerous Cloakroom*, her first full-length collection, was published by Shoestring Press in October 2006. *Taking Flight* followed in 2012.

Robert Etty was born in Lincolnshire and lives near Louth, where he taught for over thirty years in a secondary school. He began to write poems in the 1980s, and his work has appeared in many literary magazines. He is the author of nine pamphlets and collections.

Sam Gardiner was born in Portadown, Co. Armagh, and has lived and worked for the last forty-five years in Grimsby and Cleethorpes. He won the National Poetry Competition in 1993, was the Lincolnshire Millennium Laureate in 1999, and won the Poetry Business Competition in 2003. His collections include *Protestant Windows* (2000), *The Night Ships* (2007) and *The Mornings After* (2010), all published by Lagan Press.

Rennie Parker's study of twentieth-century poets was published by the British Council *Writers and their Work* series in 1999, and her poetry has appeared in magazines since 1987. Shoestring published her recent collections *Borderville* (2011) and *Candleshoe* (2014). She has two e-novellas on Kindle, appears at regional festivals, and is writing towards a booklet collection, *The Complete Electric Artisan.*

Joel Stickley is the Poet Laureate for Lincolnshire and author of the book *100 Ways to Write Badly Well*. His work has been published by Penguin, Hamish Hamilton and Pan Macmillan, as well as appearing on BBC One, BBC Radio 4 and Channel 4. With Luke Wright, he co-wrote the film *Crash! Bang! Wallow!* which won the NFBC Short Film Award at the 2010 Cannes Film Festival. With Ian McMillan, Gillian Clarke and Liz Lochhead, he wrote *Golden Fables*, a poetry theatre production inspired by the folklore of Lincolnshire.

Rory Waterman was born in Belfast in 1981, and mainly grew up near Nocton, seven miles south-east of Lincoln. He is Lecturer in English and Creative Writing at Nottingham Trent University, and co-edits *New Walk*. His debut collection, *Tonight the Summer's Over* (Carcanet, 2013), was a Poetry Book Society Recommendation and was shortlisted for the Seamus Heaney Prize. He also writes regularly for the *TLS* and other publications, has written two critical books on twentieth-century poetry, and edited *A W.H. Davies Reader* (Carcanet, 2015).